ANXIOUS
ATTACHMENT
RECOVERY

ANXIOUS
ATTACHMENT
RECOVERY

Your Complete Guide & Workbook to a
Secure Style, Moving Beyond Trauma & How
to Stop Overthinking Your Relationships

LILA HART

TABLE OF CONTENTS

INTRODUCTION

H ave you ever wondered why you struggle so much to trust people? Why you always picture how someone is going to hurt you long before the relationship has even started? Or how about why you just cannot seem to get out of this perpetual cycle of always falling for the wrong person? What about fearing being vulnerable with someone because you feel like they may use it as a weapon against you later on?

Why do we do that?

Attachment Style. That's the answer. Well, it's one of the answers. In this book, I am going to introduce you to attachment theory, which explains how we, as human beings, form attachments. It starts long before you may think and has a lasting impact on various aspects of your life. There will be moments when you sit back after reading a section in this book and think to yourself, "That's it! That's exactly how I've been feeling."

Our ability to emotionally attach to others is vital to our survival. Most other mammals are able to walk and feed themselves from the day they are born. We can't do anything for ourselves. When you are born, you're this ultra-vulnerable little lump that needs someone to do everything for you except breathe, urinate, and move your bowels. You need someone to feed you, clothe you, bathe you, burp you, and change your diapers. These are the basics for your survival.

Thanks to that big brain of yours, you start developing more complex emotional needs as you get older. You need comfort, kindness, nurturing, compassion, attentiveness, and love. You need it from the get-go, but now you are starting to form emotional attachments and beginning to understand what it feels like not to have your emotional needs met.

Unfortunately, not all of us are lucky enough to be born into homes that can provide for our emotional needs. Some of you have had to learn how to take care of yourselves from a very young age. You were treated in ways that made you believe certain things about yourself. Bad things. These experiences and beliefs have been accompanying you through life like a haunting ghost, always interfering with your relationships.

This book is the tool that will help you finally get rid of that ghost. In these pages, I will share with you all the information you need to better understand attachment theory, the different attachment styles, and how to identify your particular attachment style. We'll take a deep dive into what it means to have an anxious attachment style and how to recognize the effects that cause you to believe certain things about yourself and the world around you.

I'll also discuss the importance of self-awareness and self-regulation. What it looks like to have the ability to regulate your own emotions and equip you with tools that will help you achieve this, so you no longer need to be a slave to your emotions.

By using the strategies and tools I give to you in this book, you'll be able to go back and identify the toxic patterns that your past has left you with. You'll have the opportunity to identify the things in your life that need changing, along with tools that will allow you to implement these changes so you can live a happier, more fulfilled, and empowered life.

I don't claim to have all the answers, but I can guarantee you that you will learn a great deal about yourself and why you are attracted to the kind of people you are, why you get sucked into toxic relationships, why you feel like it's impossible to stand up for yourself, and how to empower yourself with the tools to finally turn your life around.

Are you ready?

Let's begin.

Chapter 1

Unpacking Attachment Theory

"Most people are only as needy as their unmet needs."

Amir Levine

hroughout your life, you will form attachments or emotional bonds with various people who become a part of your life in one way or another, whether it's a lover, a friend, or a family member. As human beings, we are wired for connection. Our very survival depends on it. Through evolution, different species have certain behaviors hardwired into their DNA for survival. A baby cries to signal that she's hungry or needs changing. Or screams to signal that she's hurt or feels like she's in danger. How the caregivers of that child respond to these cues will greatly impact the child's overall development. We now know that so much of what shapes us as adults comes from our early childhood experiences. But have you ever stopped to consider if the way you form emotional attachments with people might be different from the way that other people form their own emotional attachments? Have you ever wondered why?

Attachment theory answers this question quite eloquently. But first, we need to understand what attachment theory is and where it comes from.

For a long time, various scientific fields have asked the question: "What makes a person turn out the way they do in adulthood?" Is it their biological makeup that includes their genetic predispositions (that cannot be controlled), or is it the environment in which they are raised? This is the "nature versus nurture" debate. After many years of various studies, we now know that nurture trumps nature and has the greatest influence on molding us into who we become as adults.

The environment you grow up in, with an emphasis on how you were treated by the adults who surrounded you, is a key indicator for predicting the kinds of things you may struggle with later in life. Things like anxiety, depression, people-pleasing tendencies, insecurity, and so much more. Your attachment style is also shaped by the bonds you form in early childhood.

Sigmund Freud, the famous (or perhaps infamous is more fitting) Austrian neurologist and father of psychoanalysis, was the first to suggest that the relationship between infant and mother has an impact on the difficulties one might experience in adulthood. However, it was British psychologist and psychiatrist John Bowlby whose work really had the greatest impact on attachment theory. For most mammalian species, the ability to form an attachment with one's mother in infancy is a predictor for survival. When there is no emotional attachment, a mother might discard or fail to provide for her baby, which would all but wipe out its chance of survival.[1]

Some scientists initially thought that it was the act of feeding that created this bond between mother and child. However, an infamous experiment conducted by Harry Harlow on "maternal deprivation" showed that comfort and care have the greatest impact on how an infant forms attachments. In the experiment, newborn rhesus monkeys were separated from their mothers and placed in a cage with two surrogate mothers made of wire. One held a bottle from which the infant could obtain nourishment, while the other was covered in soft cloth. The experiment showed that although the infant would go to the wire mother with the bottle for food, it would always go to the soft-cloth mother for comfort. It would spend most of its time with the soft-cloth mother, showing that the need for nurturing and comfort was greater than the need for nourishment. When frightened, the monkey would always turn to the cloth-mother for comfort and protection.

This experiment solidified Bowlby's attachment theory and showed that early emotional attachments resulted from receiving care and comfort from a caregiver, not just from being fed.[2]

It's also important to note that this care does not just relate to the care you might have received from your mother when you were growing up. It's the care and fulfillment of your needs that you receive as a child, no matter who it comes from. Maybe the care, protection, and nurturing came from your father, meaning that you will have formed a stronger emotional bond with him than with your mother. Or perhaps it's both parents, or an aunt or an uncle.

Next in the line of attachment theorists came American-Canadian psychologist Mary Ainsworth. She was a prominent figure in the field of developmental psychology and came up with the "strange situation experiment" in the 1970s. The standardized procedure she developed enables one to observe the type of attachment security between an infant and his or her primary caregiver. In the original experiments, the child's mother was used as the primary caregiver.

The procedure consists of three elements: the mother, the child, and a stranger. There are eight "episodes" in which these three elements are either introduced or separated from one another. First, an observer introduces the mother and child to a room. The observer then leaves, leaving the mother and child alone for a few minutes. Then, a stranger is introduced. After a few minutes, the mother leaves the room, leaving the child with the stranger. The stranger then leaves, leaving the child alone for a few minutes. Then, the mother comes back, and finally, the mother leaves, and the stranger is left with the child again for a few minutes.[3]

The premise of the experiment was that the type of attachment style the child had with his or her mother would predict how he or she would respond to a stranger or when left alone.

Observers of the experiment focused on four elements:

✧ The child's willingness to explore.

✧ Separation anxiety.

✧ Stranger anxiety.

✧ Reunion behavior.

From these experiments, Ainsworth was able to identify three separate attachment styles.

1. Secure.

2. Avoidant.

3. Anxious.

4. Disorganized (was added later through with more research being done in the field).

Now, let's have a look at each of these four attachment styles. I want you to try to identify which one you associate with the most. This section is here to give you a starting point from which you can begin to identify your own attachment style.

It's worth noting that there is a spectrum of each attachment style, and that one *can* change their attachment style later in life. I discuss effective communication tools and strategies in Chapter 7 that will help you better connect with your partner, no matter their attachment style. Effective communication skills is beneficial in all areas of relationships whether you have an insecure attachment style or not.

The Four Attachment Styles

1. Secure Attachment Style

A parent or caregiver doesn't have to do everything 100% perfectly to ensure a child has the best chance of forming a secure attachment style. In fact, it's been shown that it's not so much the care, education, or even love given, but rather the nonverbal communication between infant and parent that creates this attachment style.[4]

We do so much of our communicating through nonverbal gestures and cues as humans, which children, especially, pick up on very easily. When a child is made to feel secure and understood, it gives them the sense that you, as the caregiver, can be trusted. This is how the attachment style begins to form.

As an example, let's say a child accidentally drops and breaks a glass. If a parent gets angry and shouts at the child for having broken a glass, they're teaching this child that it's not okay to make mistakes. Making a mistake means you're a bad child. With the child's limited emotional regulation and reasoning skills, they're forced to use the little information that's available to them. In this instance, the conclusion that is formed is that "If I make a mistake, it is bad, and it upsets mom/dad. I must be perfect; otherwise, I am not worth loving." This makes the child feel insecure and ashamed, which leads to a non-secure attachment style.

On the other hand, if that same parent looked at the child in an understanding manner, then this signals that it's okay to make mistakes . It's just a glass that can be easily replaced and teaching the child that mistakes are learning opportunities to learn from will them develop a growth mindset. What difference do you think this response would've had on the forming of the child's attachment style?

Children who are allowed to play and express themselves freely without having to be fearful of retribution when making mistakes will feel more secure within themselves and place greater trust in their relationships with their parents or primary caregivers.

As you can see, it's not so much about what people do, but how they make us feel that influences our type of attachment style. No matter how much they are loved, children who experience emotional disconnection from their primary caregiver are likely to feel uncertain, confused, unsafe, and unbalanced. So, more than anything else, it's about emotional connection and a parent tending to a child's nonverbal communication that signals their needs.

In adulthood, a secure attachment style will help you practice being a more empathic individual who is balanced and secure enough within themselves to set and enforce healthy boundaries with others. Someone with this type of attachment style tends to feel safer, more satisfied, and more stable in their relationships.

2. Avoidant Attachment Style.

Also known as "dismissive attachment", this type of attachment style usually develops in cases where at least one parent or caregiver exhibits the type of behavior that makes a child feel unsafe or fearful, like the parent who shouted at their child for accidentally dropping a glass on the floor (and does so consistently).

The type of treatment of a child that leads them to develop this attachment style can range from outright abuse to more subtle forms of neglect or trauma, causing a child to feel unsafe, confused, or unsure of themselves and their environment. Parents who are generally emotionally unavailable, neglect, or ignore their children's needs are to blame for this type of attachment style developing in their children.

For example:

John's father was an investment banker on Wall Street when he was growing up. His father's attention was only ever given to his all-important job and weekend golf outings with his banker buddies, and he rarely interacted with his son. John's mother was also neglected by his emotionally unavailable father, which led to her seeking solace in the bottom of the various wine bottles she hoped would soothe her aching heart. Ironically, the love and attention she craved from her husband is the same love and attention she withheld from her son. She treated John as more of a nuisance than anything else. This meant that John grew up learning that he could not count on others for anything and that he could only rely on himself in this world.

People with an avoidant attachment style tend to have a positive view of themselves while having a negative or skeptical view of others. This usually relates to someone who is independent and does not seek or need the support or validation of others. They also do not like others to be dependent on them. They like to be self-sufficient and can be a hard nut to crack.

Those who have developed this type of attachment style also tend to come across as quite cold or unemotional and will start to withdraw from a relationship if they feel like someone is too clingy or has become too reliant on them. Although they have a deep desire for intimacy (because they never received it in childhood), they have learned that others cannot be trusted to provide what they need.

When a child grows up with parents who pay them no attention or who are emotionally unavailable, ignore their needs, or make them feel like they're a nuisance, it causes them to feel like they must not be worthy of love and attention. When they experience this consistently, they develop a low sense of self-esteem. Every time they get shut down by a parent when trying to communicate their needs, it teaches them that they'll always get hurt when trying to connect with someone they care about. It takes a great deal for someone with an avoidant attachment style to open themselves up or trust another person, so they are also extremely sensitive to rejection. Because they equate intimacy with a loss of independence, they generally avoid intimate relationships and become overly independent. Instead of risking potentially getting hurt, they would rather keep their distance to ensure their own safety.

Because of this, a partner with this attachment style may seem to send you mixed signals. Deep down, they want to be vulnerable enough to allow themselves to be intimate with someone, but the underlying programming they received in childhood prevents them from doing so. This constant fear of being hurt, betrayed, or shut down causes them to always keep their significant other at arm's length-- if they even allow themselves to have a relationship with someone else. They might also seem oblivious to their partner's needs as they don't know what it looks like to have their own needs met by someone else. Their love life might resemble that of a string of casual relationships.

Being in a romantic relationship with someone who suffers from an avoidant attachment style can be challenging, to say the least.[5]

3. Anxious Attachment Style.

Also known as "preoccupied attachment," this is the opposite of the avoidant attachment style.

It usually develops as a result of a parent or caregiver who is not consistent in their treatment of a child, leading to them feeling unsure of both themselves and their environment. This may look like a parent who is attentive and sensitive to their child's needs at times but then emotionally unavailable, insensitive, and even cold at other times. There's no consistency, which leaves the child feeling confused and insecure. Parents who do not pick their baby or child up when they cry because they believe it's "spoiling" the child may contribute to that child developing this particular attachment style, as an example.

Another factor that may contribute to someone developing this style is repeated experiences of trauma throughout childhood, which, again, can make a child feel unsure and unsafe while growing up.

For example:

Alison's mother is a single parent who suffers from anxiety and depression. As a result, there are times when she feels like she just doesn't have the energy to attend to Alison's crying, leaving the toddler to cry out for her mother for hours on end. However, there are other days when her mother feels better and more capable of taking care of Alison, spending time with her, playing with her, and nurturing her. As you may imagine, this is terribly confusing to a toddler and makes Alison anxious when separated from her mother because she's not sure when or if her mother will return.

In adulthood, someone with this attachment style will generally struggle with a sense of self as well as a desperate need for intimacy. They always need their partner to be responsive and pay attention to them because they did not receive this consistently growing up. When this doesn't happen, they can become obsessed with the relationship, and be demanding and desperate for reassurance.

They constantly need outside approval and validation, and when they do not get it they become very insecure, leading to maladaptive behaviors that ultimately sabotage the relationship.

Where those with an avoidant attachment style tend to steer clear of romantic relationships, adults with an anxious attachment style are constantly seeking validation from their partners, leading them to very easily (and often too quickly) enter into intimate relationships. They can also easily become too dependent on their partner, as they will give up all they have just to feel loved, needed, and important to someone.

Because they have this deep need to not upset their partner, out of a fear of abandonment, they become overly sensitive to their partner's actions and moods, which in turn causes them to react in an overly emotional manner. They never learned how to regulate their emotions, set healthy boundaries, or communicate effectively, so they might become moody or unpredictable when upset. People who use tactics such as passive-aggressiveness or the silent treatment are classic examples of someone who might suffer from an anxious attachment style. This is generally due to the fact that they do not know what to do with their intense emotional reactions that stem from a fear of their partner leaving them. If this happened, it would ultimately solidify their belief that they're not worthy of love or attention.

This can often lead to a perpetual cycle of this person entering into one relationship after another, believing that if they do more, it'll make their partner love them enough not to leave them. People who find themselves in toxic, narcissistic, or physically abusive relationships usually suffer from an anxious attachment style.[6] They are often stuck in a relationship where they feel like they cannot leave because of this deep-seated need for love whilst simultaneously believing they're not worthy of it and that no one else would want to be in a relationship with them.

4. Disorganized Attachment Style.

Also known as "fearful-avoidant", this particular style develops in response to a parent's consistent failure to respond (or respond in an appropriate manner) to a child's needs and feelings of fear or distress.

Parents who tend to use fear, intimidation tactics, mockery, or outright ignoring their child usually cause this type of attachment style to develop as the child is constantly exposed to different types of trauma and abuse. It causes the child to live in fear and feel unsure of themselves and others.

For example:

Dave is an orphan who has been passed off from one foster home to the next. The people who have taken him in have predominantly been adults who take foster children in so they can profit off the government grants that come with adopting a foster child. They don't really care about taking care of his needs.

Most of the homes that Dave has had the misfortune of being placed in exposed him to a great deal of neglect and violence, with foster parents who use intimidation and tactics of physical abuse to show Dave "who's the boss." As a result, Dave grew up without knowing what it meant to be cared for; he always needed to look out for himself, take care of himself, and not be able to trust anyone.

In adulthood, someone like Dave can live with a strong fear of others hurting him if he allows himself to be vulnerable. As with the avoidant attachment style, those suffering from a disorganized attachment style will often refrain from entering into romantic or close relationships because of the deep-seated fear of trusting others and getting hurt that they struggle with. The difference is that those who have developed this disorganized attachment style *want* to be in a relationship, whereas, with an avoidant attachment style, the person doesn't care for close relationships.

Someone like Dave may be hard to predict when it comes to his behavior in an adult intimate relationship. Because there's a constant yo-yoing of feelings where he wants to be in a loving relationship but fears being hurt, he appears to be "disorganized" or not knowing what he wants. He might often struggle to believe someone when they tell him that they love or care for him because the experiences he had in all those foster homes taught him that he's unlovable and just an asset to be passed around for others' benefit. So, he may be very clingy one moment and then suddenly come across as distant as he struggles with this internal turmoil that is constantly present.

Because we so often seek out what we're familiar with, Dave may also seek out relationships with individuals who are abusive and unstable, recreating the environment he's come to know so well. He may pick fights with his partner or completely shut down during arguments, again displaying this *disorganized* attachment style that he's developed.[7]

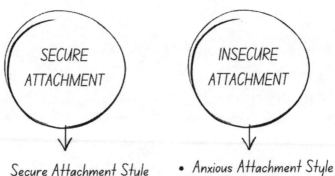

- Secure Attachment Style
- Anxious Attachment Style
- Avoidant Attachment Style
- Disorganized Attachment Style

Recognizing Your Attachment Style

Knowing what signs to look for will help you identify your attachment style. Go through all the signs associated with each of the attachment styles and try to identify which style you equate your own behavior in relationships with.

1. **Secure Attachment**

   ✧ Enjoy intimate relationships.

   ✧ Positive self-esteem.

   ✧ Comfortable in close, warm, loving relationships.

   ✧ Easy to connect with.

   ✧ Comfortable being yourself around others.

   ✧ Comfortable sharing emotions.

   ✧ Strong emotional regulation skills.

   ✧ Able to handle conflict well.

   ✧ An ability to seek out comfort when in need.

   ✧ Open and honest with your partner.

   ✧ There's a great sense of trust in your relationship/s.

   ✧ You support your partner and know you can rely on them when needed.

   ✧ Sensitive, warm, caring.

   ✧ You easily trust others.

   ✧ Comfortable being on your own, and do not experience separation anxiety when your partner is not with you.

   ✧ You view both yourself and others in a positive light.

   ✧ You're empathic, tolerant of differences, understanding, and forgiving.

2. **Avoidant Attachment**

   ✧ You avoid letting people get too close to you, i.e., emotional connection.

   ✧ You're highly independent and believe you don't need other people in your life.

- ✧ You have a hard time trusting people.

- ✧ You're emotionally distant and don't share personal details with others.

- ✧ You struggle with maintaining any long-term relationships.

- ✧ The thought of intimacy makes you fear losing your independence.

- ✧ Your communication tends to be more intellectual than emotional.

- ✧ You tend to spend more time on your own than with others.

- ✧ You are often dismissive of others.

- ✧ You find it hard to "lean on" your partner or to ask for help. You'd rather do it yourself than feel like you "owe" someone for doing something for you.

- ✧ You're someone who's good in a crisis; because you're not emotional, it allows you to take charge.

- ✧ As a parent, you are emotionally unavailable.

3. Anxious Attachment

- ✧ Clingy tendencies.

- ✧ You struggle with a fear of abandonment.

- ✧ You can be overly sensitive to your partner's moods and behaviors.

- ✧ You crave constant attention and validation from your partner.

- ✧ You can become overly fixated on a relationship.

- ✧ Unpredictable and moody.

- ✧ You tend to ruminate on the past, constantly blaming it for your current struggles and behavior.

- ✧ Low self-esteem.

- ✧ Struggles with jealousy.

- ✧ You're sensitive to criticism and have an intense fear of rejection.
- ✧ You find it difficult to trust others.
- ✧ You struggle with emotional regulation and can sometimes become quite combative.
- ✧ You are inconsistent in your attachment to your children.
- ✧ You can't be alone.

4. Disorganized Attachment

- ✧ You hold onto past traumas and pain that have not yet been resolved.
- ✧ Difficulty trusting others.
- ✧ Your close and romantic relationships tend to be quite dysfunctional.
- ✧ You struggle with high levels of anxiety.
- ✧ Your emotions can go from love to hate in a short period of time.
- ✧ Narcissistic behavior.
- ✧ You come across as unemotional with a lack of empathy for others.
- ✧ Likely to mistreat your own children.
- ✧ You feel unworthy of love or adoration.
- ✧ You display signs of both avoidant and anxious attachment styles.
- ✧ You may suffer from a mental illness/es.[8]

Looking at the signs described above, can you recognize any of your own struggles in any of them? Are you able to identify which attachment style you hold, personally? Once you are able to identify your personal attachment style, you can start working on identifying the areas in your life that are most impacted by symptoms related to your attachment style. Then comes the inner work of understanding what caused you to adopt this particular attachment style and what you need to do to resolve any trauma or pain from your past.

The Impact of Insecure Attachment

Someone who didn't grow up in a secure, consistent, and supportive home environment will more often than not develop an insecure attachment style. As you can see from the examples above, this can tremendously impact one's relationships and quality of life.

The good news is that you can learn how to change your behaviors going forward. Nothing is set in stone, and you can always choose to change your situation. It will take time and a lot of inner work but knowing that you have a choice can be extremely empowering. You can choose what you allow yourself to focus on, what beliefs you decide to hold onto, how to regulate your emotions, and the behaviors you allow yourself to exhibit.

This is excellent news as it means that you do not have to be a slave to these underlying beliefs and insecurities imparted to you by people from your past. You can heal yourself and take charge of your own life.

We all need significant and emotional attachments with others. Even though an insecure attachment style might make it challenging for you to trust others enough to be vulnerable and allow them close to you, all is not lost. With time, you can learn how to recognize when someone is trustworthy and secure enough within themselves to allow you to be vulnerable with them without fear of judgment, criticism, or abandonment.

Being stuck in an insecure relationship can be dangerous to your health, physically, mentally, and emotionally. This is why it's so important to understand what it is you need to work on to become more secure within yourself so you no longer feel the need to enter these types of relationships.

You owe it to yourself to invest in your own growth and well-being. You owe it to yourself to have secure, caring, trusting, and fulfilling relationships with the people in your life. This includes any potential romantic partners and children you have or might have in the future.

Your particular attachment style will impact every aspect of your life. Not just can, it *will*. It will impact how you identify with and respond to others. The type of romantic partners you seek out and enter into a relationship with. The way you regulate (or don't) your emotions and conduct yourself in general. How you raise your children. How you treat them on a daily basis. How you deal with challenges. Whether you develop symptoms of anxiety or depression. And so much more.

As we discuss anxious attachment in greater depth in the following chapter, along with the science behind why we adopt certain beliefs and behaviors, you'll also be equipped with the knowledge and tools on how to break the chains that may have been holding you hostage up until now.

In the following chapters, I will introduce you to a number of tools and strategies that you can use to help you on your healing journey. First, let's delve deeper into the subject of anxious attachment.

EXERCISE

(If you're reading this book in its electronic format, I suggest writing down your answers on a piece of paper or using a separate tablet or a computer. You can also use the notes function on your device if it has that functionality)

Go through the signs of the different attachment styles in this chapter and write down all the signs you identify with. Then, consider which attachment style your list fits best.

_____

_____

_____

_____

_____

_____

Can you identify any experiences in childhood that may have led to you developing your specific attachment style? Write them down here.

_____

_____

_____

_____

_____

_____

_____

Chapter 2

Anxious Attachment: in-Depth

"That's the tricky thing about the anxiously attached person, they're so ahead of being abandoned that they abandon themselves over and over and over again."

Michelle Panning

N
ow that you have a better idea of the causes and signs of the different types of attachment styles, let's delve deeper into and unpack anxious attachment so you are able to understand and recognize it even better and more easily.

A Deep Dive Into Anxious Attachment

As we now know, the way we behave in our relationships as adults bears a direct correlation with the way we were cared for as infants.

Anxious attachment is rooted in the fear of abandonment and one's need for appreciation. People who suffer from anxious attachment often struggle with their own sense of identity and self-worth.

It is estimated that roughly 20% of people suffer from an anxious attachment style.

If you consider the meaning of the word "anxious," what comes to mind? Feeling unsure? Feeling unsafe? Feeling unbalanced or insecure? Feeling fearful? These are exactly the kinds of insecurities someone who suffers from anxious attachment carries with them. They were never shown or taught what secure emotional attachment looks like. Without self-awareness, this can cause one to go through life without ever finding an answer to the question, *"Why do I struggle with the things I struggle with in my relationships?"*

Unless you know what the problem is, you can't possibly find a solution, can you? Or should I say, first, you need to recognize that there is a problem. Then, figure out what the problem is and how to fix it.

What is it that "attaches" us to other people? Think about it for a second. What makes you feel "attached" to someone? And, what need drives that attachment?

The definition of the word "attach" is to connect, link, join, or secure. We "connect" with and "attach" to others to fulfill certain human needs. These needs vary from companionship to procreation, friendship, emotional connection, sharing of interests, physical needs, desire, understanding, protection, and so much more.

Let's consider Jane. She grew up as an only child in a household filled with alcoholics. Both her mother, father, and grandparents all lived under one roof, along with Jane. The adults around her used alcohol as a way to self-medicate in order to escape their own emotions connected to traumas from their past. Even though they always made sure Jane was clean, clothed, and fed, they paid little else attention to her. When she cried, she was scolded. She found herself in a typical "children are to be seen, not heard" type of scenario, which is a pretty abusive motto in its own right.

Jane spent most of her time alone as she got older. No one ever played with her, and she wasn't allowed in the company of adults. She was never allowed to voice her own opinions or have friends over. The only time she received any kind of recognition was when she brought a gleaming report card home or when she did something really well.

What do you think this kind of treatment taught Jane? What impact would it have had on the type of attachment style she'd eventually form?

Would it teach her that she's not worthy of attention? That in order to gain someone's love or attention, she has to be perfect? That she's not allowed to speak up for herself? That she's not worthy of having her own opinions? That no one cares about her needs, interests, or wants?

How do you think this might turn into an anxious attachment style, and how do you think it might materialize in her adult relationships?

I'd say that Jane probably grows up to be an overachiever because, subconsciously, she has been taught to believe that she has to be exceptional or perfect to earn someone's attention, affection, and love. She might struggle with emotional dysregulation and moodiness in her relationships because she was never taught how to regulate herself. Perhaps she gets overly clingy when she finds someone who showers her with affection and love because it's what she's been yearning for all her life. Or maybe she comes across as cut off, emotionally, because it's all she's ever known.

Do you see how these early childhood experiences form attachment styles that have a long-lasting impact on us and our relationships?

An anxious attachment style can sabotage not only your and your partner's happiness, but also your ability to live in and appreciate the present. An anxious attachment style causes people to forever be on the lookout for evidence of looming danger or evidence that their partner is cheating on them, doesn't love them, doesn't care enough, doesn't pay enough attention to them, etc. Instead of focusing on and being present in your relationship, this constantly raises questions and issues about small details that don't really matter.[9]

So often, the very thing someone is trying to avoid (abandonment) happens *because* of their behavior. They don't want their partner to end the relationship (abandon them), so they become overly invested and clingy, and suffocate the relationship to death, leading their partner to leave. Which is the very thing they feared and tried to avoid. This, of course, now only cements the idea in their mind that they are not worthy, and that people will always abandon them. People who are anxiously attached to others often come across as emotionally needy individuals. This is usually off-putting, except for narcissists who prey on the emotionally vulnerable.

Furthermore, those with an anxious attachment style will often attract someone with an avoidant attachment style as they identify in one another the emotional needs that they have longed for since childhood. As we now know, people with an anxious attachment style tend to go after reassurance and closeness from their significant other, whereas someone with an avoidant attachment style needs to feel independent and self-reliant. An anxious attacher's constant pursuit of validation and closeness may cause the avoidant attacher to feel like they don't have to put in much effort and that this person won't leave them because of their *"neediness."* The avoidant attacher may also seek out what the anxious attacher has to give because they feel like they might be missing out on what they actually really want: unconditional love and acceptance. That's mostly what we all want, wouldn't you agree?

And so the vicious cycle continues.

That is, until someone stops and takes a step back to assess what is causing this cycle to repeat itself. The next step is to go back and look at how experiences in their past may have brought them to this point and what they can do about it.

Recognizing Patterns from the Past

It is only through practicing self-awareness on a continuous basis that we enable ourselves to identify patterns of behavior that are not helpful to us in our lives. Once you're able to pinpoint what it is that's not working in your life or causing trouble in your relationships, you can trace it to its source by asking questions like, "What happened in the past that made me believe this?" or, "What emotions cause me to react in this manner?"

As a child, you know very little of this world. Everything you know is based on how you get treated by the people charged with taking care of you. That's why survivors of abuse so often struggle with imposter syndrome because they feel like what they experienced was *"normal."* It *was* their normal . That is until they started interacting with other children and adults and realizing that others' lives looked so different from theirs. What they'd accepted as normal all their lives might not be normal after all. Or perhaps it would be better to substitute the word "normal" with "healthy," as *normal* can be such a relative term.

To uncover the behavioral changes you need to make, you need to follow that path back all the way to the experience or instance that first caused you to feel something that triggered the behavior that's now causing you struggles and grief in adulthood.

Considering your own characteristics and the difficulties or challenges you tend to experience in your adult relationships will give you a good starting point to work from.

For example:

Let's say that you struggle with jealousy. You have always struggled with jealousy in your relationships. You hate the fact that you struggle with this emotion, but it feels impossible to overcome. Ask yourself, "Where did this come from?" Do you think there might be an instance or repeated instances in your childhood that might have led to you struggling with this emotion?

How has this affected the relationships you've had up until now? I'd take an educated guess and say that it has caused some difficulties with your previous partners. Pushing them away because you feel like you don't trust them? Do you think that is the real reason why you struggle with jealousy? Because you don't trust people? And, if that is the case, why do you think that is?

This is how we start to understand how our childhood experiences may have impacted the difficulties we tend to experience in our relationships now in adulthood.

Suppose you struggle with a fear of abandonment due to parents or primary caregivers who were never consistent in their caregiving. In that case, it may have led you to come across as "clingy" or "desperate" in your relationships. You may not have been able to connect the dots up until now. There is also the possibility that you naturally developed a fear of abandonment due to some underlying cause related to mental illness. You'd still need to investigate your past from a different angle. As an example, children who develop borderline personality disorder at a young age may also tend to come across as clingy, anxious, and afraid of being left alone. In this instance, your inherited genes are to blame more than the environment you grew up in.

Although suffering from an anxious attachment style isn't technically a disorder and is not listed in the DSM-V-TR (The Diagnostic and Statistical Manual of Mental Disorders), symptoms of anxious attachment can sometimes be associated with:

- ✧ **Borderline Personality Disorder**: This causes an individual to suffer from intense emotions and an intense fear of abandonment–whether real or imagined.

✧ **Substance Use Disorders**: Substance use can alter one's brain chemistry, which has an impact on one's ability to rationalize and execute critical thinking. It can make one feel paranoid or suspicious of scenarios that only exist in the mind and can often present as an anxious attachment.

✧ **Social Anxiety Disorder**: Someone who is diagnosed with SAD experiences high levels of anxiety and feels like others are constantly judging them. Their symptoms of chronically elevated anxiety levels may lead them to fall victim to negative thinking patterns and develop an anxious attachment style.

And, of course, stress and trauma experienced outside of the home environment may also play a role in someone developing an anxious attachment style. Any instance where a child is exposed to an experience that leaves them feeling unsafe or unsure adds to the potentiality of them developing anxiety and an anxious attachment style.[10]

The upcoming exercise will help you to identify instances and lessons from your past that may have influenced your particular attachment style. It's important to note that no one person displays 100% of the same attachment style 100% of the time. We all tend to move between different attachment styles depending on the type of relationship we find ourselves in. Besides, not all relationships are the same. However, you should have been able to identify the one you predominantly associate with within the section we covered about recognizing your own attachment style in Chapter 1.

Questions to ask yourself:

What did your family teach you about vulnerability and emotions?

Were you taught how to regulate your own emotions?

_____

_____

Did you have to internalize your emotions because you weren't allowed to express yourself, or did you feel safe to show how you felt?

_____

_____

Did the adults around you label emotions as good or bad?

_____

_____

Did your parents or caregivers show emotion freely?

_____

_____

Did you feel supported when you expressed how you felt?

_____

_____

What have your culture and religion taught you about emotions?

_____

_____

Does your culture value independence? If not, what does it value instead?

_____

_____

What were you taught about cultural differences growing up?

_____

_____

Were your parents or caregivers consistent in their behavior and treatment of you? If not, explain.

_____

_____

Who did you turn to for comfort and support as a child?

_____

_____

Who do you turn to for comfort and support now?

_____

_____

What does comfort and support look like to you?

_____

_____

Ask a few friends (or ask the question on social media) what comfort and support look like to them and compare it to your answer.

_____

_____

Do you feel like you can find comfort and support within yourself? If not, explain why not.

_____

_____

Did you feel like you could ask for what you needed in childhood? Explain why or why not.

_____

_____

Do you turn to people or substances for support? Why?

_____

_____

What made you feel like you were loved as a child?

_____

_____

Are you able to allow yourself to receive love, and what makes you feel loved now as an adult?

_____

_____

How do you show others love?

_____

_____

What makes you feel uncomfortable in your relationships?

_____

_____

How do you communicate your discomfort?

_____

_____

How do your relationships generally tend to end? Do you leave people, or do they leave you?

_____

_____

Do you tend to stay in relationships even when they are no longer healthy to you? If yes, why?

_____

_____

How do you deal with feeling overwhelmed emotionally?

_____

_____

[11]

Take some time to consider your answers to these questions. Perhaps you may have experienced some "aha" moments where you realized why you feel certain things or react in certain ways now in your adult relationships. Perhaps not. That's okay too. This is a good way of posing probing questions to yourself so you can explore the origins of certain emotions and behaviors you either struggle with or which cause some kind of struggle in your relationships or life in general. Following on from the exercise you did in Chapter 1, try to identify any new clues you may have uncovered in this last exercise and write them down in your journal. If you don't have a journal, get one, as I'll be sharing some helpful journaling exercises for inner healing later on.

Understanding the Anxious Mind

The anxious mind is quite often an equation that looks like this:

Overestimating danger + Underestimating self-confidence = Anxious Mind

Some people may confuse anxiety with stress. However, they're two different emotions caused by different circumstances. Where stress is normally associated with a clear "trigger", anxiety can often occur without there being a clear indication as to why it's happening. However, there are usually clues that can help you solve the puzzle of why you feel the way you feel.

How you interpret things: This tends to significantly impact how you view yourself and the world around you. Someone with an anxious mind or a mind wired to react more anxiously will often view the world in a more negative or threatening way, even when there is no reason to do so. For example, when someone comments saying, "Those are interesting shoes you are wearing," which is an ambiguous comment, an anxious mind will tend to interpret it as being negative.

Someone who suffers from low self-esteem and who tends to be more sensitive to others' behaviors will constantly scan their environment to try and ascertain what others are thinking, even though it's impossible. If someone happens to look at them for too long (due to maybe just being lost in thought), they might interpret that as this person judging them. It's easy to see how this constant trying to ascertain and predict what others are thinking and how they might react can perpetuate feelings of anxiety and strengthen emotions that lead to false beliefs. Thoughts are just information that constantly pop into your mind. We may not be able to control these thoughts, but we can control what information we allow into our heads, and influence those thoughts.

Thoughts are just thoughts, not facts.

Worrying About the Future: It's normal to try and predict the future, and to worry about what we need to do now in order to reach a good one. Unfortunately, we do not have crystal balls and no way of knowing what the future holds. Every second that passes has the potential to change your future completely.

This uncertainty can make someone with an anxious mind fall into the trap of worrying persistently. Worrying is brought on by a need to problem solve. Problem-solving is brought on by a need to control one's environment. If you cannot control what happens around you or predict what will happen to you in the future, it causes stress. It's normal for most of us to stress about the future, but for someone with a mind that's wired for anxious thinking, it means ruminating on all the negative or bad things that could potentially happen. Which just causes more anxiety.

There's this thing known as the ironic effects of mental control which teaches us that the more you try not to worry, the more you will worry. It's a bit like telling someone not to think of a pink elephant, and one immediately pops into their head.

Negative moods are often caused by incessant worrying and feeling anxious about things you cannot control. Although some might say, "So just focus on something else," it's easier said than done. For those who suffer from low to moderate levels of anxiety, this might be possible with some training and practicing self-awareness, but for those who suffer from an anxiety disorder, a more professional approach is needed by way of therapy. The difference between the two is that one may feel anxious from time to time, whereas someone with an anxiety disorder suffers from very high levels of anxiety every single day, and it negatively influences their ability to live a productive life.[12]

Cognitive Distortions: These are beliefs and biases we hold without really considering how factual and helpful they are. All the experiences we have throughout life contribute toward us forming certain beliefs and holding certain values. Cognitive distortions are like filters we view the world through. If your filter is negative, the way you view the world will also be negative. Being aware of and fixing these distortions can really help improve the quality of your life and relationships. The concept of cognitive distortions is rooted in Cognitive Behavioral Therapy (CBT), which is considered the gold standard of therapeutic frameworks used today by mental health professionals the world over.

Here are some examples of cognitive distortions. See if you can identify any of these in yourself.

Mindreading: Assuming that you know what someone else is thinking. We never truly know what others are thinking. We may be able to try and guess what they're thinking, but unless you know someone intimately, it'll end up being wrong more often than not. An example of how this can have a negative impact on your life is when you form a conclusion about what someone thinks of you based on an interaction that turns out to be not true at all. You may react in a way that is influenced by your initial conclusion, which then has a negative impact on the relationships. Let's say, for example, that Alison gets to the office and greets her boss. Her boss doesn't greet her back the way she usually does. Because Alison suffers from an anxious mind due to her anxious attachment style, she may think that her boss is upset with her because she didn't greet her when she usually always greets her. Is she right in thinking that her boss is upset with her? Of course not. There could be so many other explanations, like perhaps she was just not paying attention or on a video call without Alison knowing it. There's no way of knowing what she was thinking without actually asking her outright.

Catastrophizing: This is when you always think of a worst-case scenario. For example, let's say Alison wants to ask someone out, and she thinks to herself, "If this person says no, it means that I am a total failure and will never find love in life." Is that true? Of course not.

Emotional Reasoning: If I FEEL it, it MUST mean that it's true. "I FEEL she likes me. This must mean she's in love with me." Or "I don't feel like I'm attractive" makes you believe that you truly are unattractive, and no one will ever find you attractive. You can see how this can cause all sorts of challenges in one's life.

Personalization: Thinking that everything is always your fault. For example, let's say Alison was running late one morning and happened to be involved in a minor vehicle collision on her way to dropping her son off at school. Although the collision was a minor one, her son broke his wrist while trying to brace himself with one hand against the dashboard. This leads Alison to think, "If only I hadn't been running late this morning, this wouldn't have happened. This is all my fault." No, it's not. There's no way of knowing that something else might not have happened had she been on time. People who have experienced abuse and trauma in childhood often tend to personalize everything that happens in their lives due to a low sense of self-esteem and certain beliefs instilled in them in childhood.[13]

These are just a few examples of the different cognitive distortions that exist. There are around 15 common cognitive distortions that you can learn more about by consulting the resources page at the back of this book.

Doing research, reading books like this one, and engaging in the exercises I've given you will help you better understand your own anxious mind and why you think the way you do. Once you are able to understand how your mind works and why, you can begin to rewire it to adopt new and more helpful thought patterns based on facts rather than fabrications your mind comes up with.

How to Identify Your Own Cognitive Distortions

Awareness, awareness, awareness. The more you practice, the more progress you'll make in becoming more self-aware. The most effective way to identify the different cognitive distortions you may be viewing the world through is to use a combination of a thought diary and a list of your personal core values. How we think about and see others around us often stems from our values and how we believe others should conduct themselves. When they don't, it might cause us to hold them in a negative light because of the filters through which we view them.

Here is a list of core values for you to go through. Circle or highlight the ones you associate with and think about where they stem from.

✧ Compassion	✧ Accountability
✧ Honesty	✧ Discipline
✧ Creativity	✧ Assertiveness
✧ Loyalty	✧ Wealth
✧ Achievement	✧ Health
✧ Balance	✧ Friendship
✧ Community	✧ Hard work
✧ Family	✧ Determination
✧ Religion	✧ Security
✧ Confidence	✧ Beauty

Thought Diary:

Keep a diary with you for the next 3 weeks. It can be a physical diary or an electronic one. Every time you become aware of yourself experiencing a negative emotion, consider the event that caused you to feel this way. Write it down, along with the thoughts you had along with these negative emotions.

Over time, you'll notice yourself becoming more self-aware and able to identify these thoughts and emotions with more ease. After 3 weeks, go through what you've written down. Seek out a more comprehensive list of cognitive distortions online and print it out or write it down. Then, take the information you now have regarding your negative thought patterns, and see if you can link it to certain cognitive distortions.

For example:

One of Alison's core beliefs is that one should always be honest. Her mother used to tell her that and would spank her whenever she did something wrong and wasn't honest about it. As such, honesty is one of Alison's core values. In the 3 weeks that she kept a thought diary, she noticed that she got really upset or felt very uncomfortable whenever someone wasn't telling the truth or lied to one another in the office. Even when it had nothing to do with her, it caused her to form certain beliefs about these people. When she looked at her diary and compared it with the list of cognitive distortions she had printed out, she was suddenly able to identify that she suffers from the ***"Should"*** distortion, which relates to believing that all people *should* conduct themselves in a certain manner.

We cannot control what others think, feel, or do. It is wise to learn to focus only on what you can control in your own life. The lives of others are none of your business really. Even when it comes to the people we are close with– allow them to have their moods without making it about yourself

Signs and Behaviors of Anxious Attachment

Signs of anxious attachment in adults typically look different from signs and behaviors of anxious attachment in children. It makes sense. As adults, our needs and interactions become far more complex than those we have in childhood.

In children, signs of anxious attachment may present as:

✧ Being inconsolable when crying, even if you try to comfort the child.

✧ Not being able to put a name to their emotions.

✧ Generally appearing to be anxious.

✧ A fear of or not interacting with strangers.

- They experience and exhibit intense emotions, more so than other children.

- Displaying aggressive behavior, especially when interacting with other children. (This usually stems from frustration because they do not know and have not been taught how to regulate their own emotions)

- Clinging to their parents or primary caregivers.

- Separation anxiety. Getting really upset when separated from their parents or other primary caregivers.

In adults, it looks more like:

- Intense jealousy.

- Low self-worth.

- A fear of abandonment.

- Being constantly suspicious of others.

- An inability to resolve conflict effectively.

- Almost clingy due to craving closeness and intimacy.

- Poor sense of personal boundaries.

- Worrying excessively.

- Catastrophizing.

- Being overly dependent in romantic relationships.

- Not being able to spend time alone or a fear of being alone.

- Needing constant reassurance from others, especially your partner.

In romantic relationships, it might come across as:

- Constantly meddling in or trying to resolve your partner's problems *for* them. (So you feel needed or trying to make yourself indispensable)

- Constantly overstepping others' boundaries.

✧ Craving attention from others.

✧ Needing constant support and validation.

✧ Intense jealousy of anyone who takes up any of your partner's time because they should be spending that time with you.

✧ A fear that your partner will leave or abandon you.

✧ Getting upset when your partner doesn't act or react the way you want them to in any given situation.[14]

As you can see, this can cause a relationship to become unstable and challenging. When someone suffers from an anxious attachment style, they're not *trying* to make things difficult on purpose. They might not even be aware of why the various relationships they hold with different people in their lives seem so strained and complicated.

It's only when you stop projecting everything onto the outside world and start looking inward with an empathic curiosity to understand yourself better that you realize there are some things you need to work on in your behavior.

Fear of Abandonment

In a sense, we all fear those we love leaving us or being taken from us. This is not what I'm referring to here. A fear of abandonment is an intense and unwarranted fear that someone you love will leave or abandon you. It often forms in children when they are brought up by parents who aren't consistent in the emotional support and love they give their child. As I mentioned previously, it could also develop as a result of a mental health struggle, which could turn into an anxiety disorder due to a genetic predisposition.[15]

Although we don't know exactly how fear of abandonment develops, there are various theories that range from abnormal development of cognitive and emotional capacities in a child to challenges in the child's environment–as in the case of unstable and unpredictable treatment by parents or other caregivers.

It can be a downright debilitating condition to deal with. Although not an officially listed phobia, it causes one to experience intense fear and negative emotions, which has a negative impact both on yourself in terms of how you think of and treat yourself and your various relationships.

This constant worry of rejection can cause you to retreat into your own little world and not take chances on what you want to achieve. For example, asking out that guy you've had a crush on for so long, applying for that new job opening, proposing something in a meeting, taking that class you've been wanting to, and so much more. It's a fear that has a toxic impact on just about every aspect of your life.

Symptoms of a fear of abandonment might look like:

✧ Feeling highly insecure and unworthy of love.

✧ Being a people pleaser.

✧ Getting attached too quickly.

✧ Being extremely sensitive to criticism.

✧ Finding it hard to trust others.

✧ Overreacting when you feel brushed off.

✧ You often engage in self-blaming.

✧ Feeling like you're not enough. Not pretty enough, not smart enough, etc.

✧ You obsessively worry about what others might think of you.

✧ You've had very few long-term relationships, mainly because you struggle to commit. (You tend to break up with someone before they break up with you)

✧ You crave intimacy but fear allowing yourself to get close to someone in case they end up hurting and leaving you.

✧ You can be very clingy, even when someone expresses to you that they need space.

✧ You always step over other people's boundaries because you need to be close to them.

Coming to understand and accept these struggles and traits you may not like so much is part and parcel of the healing process. What's crucial is that you cut yourself some slack. No one is perfect. We all have different things in our lives that need work.

Any type of personal development work should always be done in partnership with a whole lot of self-compassion. There's absolutely no judgment allowed, as it's counter-productive. We are all fallible beings, and mistakes are good. Being able to identify what it is you need to work on to become a better version of yourself is good. It's a beautiful opportunity you grant yourself. Few people are willing to take a look in the mirror and identify the parts of themselves that might have been the cause of the troubles they've experienced in their past and current relationships. So, you should give yourself a big pat on the back. This is hard work. But oh, so worth it.

In the next chapter, we'll take a deep dive into the science behind attachment and what the research that's available has come up with in terms of explaining the ins and outs of how and why attachment forms.

Chapter 3

The Science Behind Attachment

"The root of suffering is attachment."

Buddha

n this chapter we will uncover the science of attachment theory, from research by leading experts to the neurobiology of attachment, and its ongoing influence throughout life. For so long the nature versus nurture debate had scientists exploring various avenues that have led to us gaining a better understanding of the different structures of the human brain, how the different areas of the brain affect our thoughts, emotions, and behaviors, and how the environments we are exposed to help shape our brains and predicting how we may behave in the future.

Without any substantial scientific evidence to back a theory, it becomes null and void. Attachment theory has stood the test of time when it comes to the vast amount of research that has been conducted on this subject over the last 50 years. Let's have a look at what the research tells us.

What Does the Research Say About Attachment Theory

There are several different questions we need to ask ourselves to establish the true validity of attachment theory as we know it. Questions like:

✧ What constitutes an attachment relationship?

✧ How do we quantify or measure the security of an attachment?

✧ How do we differentiate how we see ourselves and the world around us and the causes these views stem from?

✧ How does attachment differ in different cultures?

✧ Are current attachment-based therapies useful or successful in helping to treat difficulties stemming from an individual's particular attachment style?

A research paper conducted by Ross. A. Thompson et al., published in the Attachment and Human Development Journal in January of 2022, invited 75 experts in various fields of psychology to answer these types of questions. They had this to say.

When looking at the question of what constitutes attachment, it brings up another question. Why should we qualify relationships like those with our parents, extended family, adult romantic partners, and friends as "attachments" and not others? The simple answer is that attachment relationships are very different from other relationships in that we seek comfort, protection, love, and support from these relationships and rely on these for our further development, whereas this is not the case for other relationships like your second cousin twice removed, for example. The attachment relationships relate to those who have the greatest impact on your early years and, of course, in adulthood, but in a more intimate way.

As far as how we should quantify or measure attachment, the question should rather be focused on assessing whether everyone's measuring the same thing within the different therapeutic areas. The simple answer is, quite emphatically, no. Various assessments and questionnaires exist, and no two of them will deliver the same outcome. The same thing goes for the same assessments conducted within different developmental periods of an individual's life. Outcomes in your tween years and outcomes in your fifties to the same assessment will differ. In the same way, outcomes from one assessment method compared to a different one will also vary. What this means is that conclusions should be made cautiously and might need further investigation before drawing a final conclusion about certain predictabilities.

How attachment is defined also differs between cultural settings. This makes it difficult to pinpoint a single definition of attachment. When you look at Western culture vs traditional African culture, attachment is formed and relies on slightly different elements. In America, the culture a child is normally brought up in is a single-family unit consisting of a father, mother, and perhaps siblings and grandparents. Many families have to rely on services like daycare or the education system to watch their children the majority of the time. In most African cultures, the upbringing of children is a communal task. All the adults in the community are charged with the care of all the children.

The next question that asks whether the various attachment therapies work is one that is difficult to answer. It would depend on who you ask. Some practitioners and their clients may experience great results, whereas others don't. So, it's really something that needs to be assessed on an individual basis. One shoe will not fit everyone's feet. We're all unique and respond differently to different therapeutic models, different environments, different therapists, etc.

There are so many other possible questions we could ask that would lead us down various different paths. If I go on, this will end up being a research paper, and that's not what this book is about. What I want to show here is that no single theory or therapy is perfect. As humans, we are very complex creatures, which makes it impossible to have just one single overarching assessment or questionnaire that will accurately predict what is needed to help someone move forward in their lives.

Having said that, attachment theory is one of the few theories in psychology that has stood the test of time where most others have fallen by the wayside and many professionals agree that it still has validity even in today's milieu. As with anything else, there are always areas that can be improved upon.[16]

The Neurobiology of Attachment

Our advanced, evolved brains cause us so much heartache. Think about it. A worm wouldn't be reading this book to work out its own attachment style, would it? Nothing against worms. They're cute (to some). My point is that our beautifully complex brains give us the ability to contemplate things like the type of attachment theory we may have, where it stems from, and what that means.

We've made great strides in mapping the brain in recent decades. People often think we haven't made that many medical or scientific discoveries in recent years. They forget that it's only in the last 50 years we've developed antibiotics, eradicated smallpox, decoded the human genome, created the MRI machine, figured out how to transplant different organs, and *so* much more.

Thanks to these advancements, we can measure certain effects of inputs in the brain. This allows us to understand better how certain variables may influence the development of different areas of the brain and how that influences an individual's thought processes, emotional responses, verbal abilities, and behavioral implications.

fMRI (functional magnetic resonance imaging) machines are now able to measure how core relationships affect the development and functioning of different areas in the brain.

While in the womb, mother and baby are connected physiologically with their heartbeat, hypothalamic-pituitary-adrenal activation, and oxytocin levels mirroring one another. Oxytocin is a hormone that plays a key role in bonding. See the diagram below for a visual representation of this process.

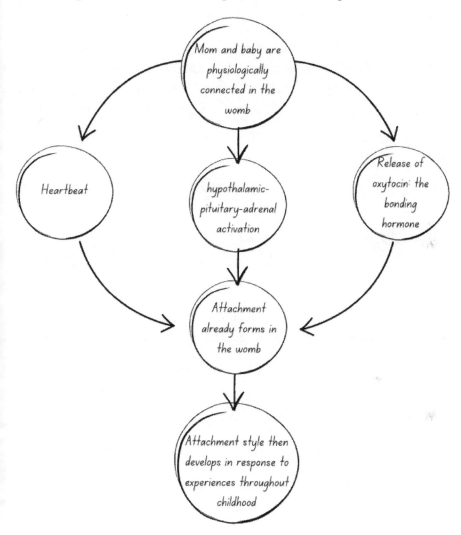

The brain's DMN (Default Mode Network), which is involved in remembering the past and envisioning the future plays a key role in storing certain experiences from childhood to assign prior probabilities to future events. In other words, if Jane is a single mother who struggles with mental illness, Sally is going to grow up with inconsistent parenting, which her

DMN will store. It will then use that information to predict that any future relationship will also make her feel abandoned or confused, leaving Sally with separation anxiety that impacts all her adulthood relationships.

The amygdala, which is responsible for activating the fight or flight response, has also been shown to develop differently in people who have experienced repeated abuse or traumas in life. This could then cause one to develop an anxiety or panic disorder, along with an anxious attachment style.

More recently, other methods like EEGs (electroencephalograms), genetic markers, endocrinological probes, and pharmacological manipulation have provided us with even more insights into the neurobiological element of attachment theory.

The fields of neurobiology and neuroscience are fascinating and truly remarkable at giving us an inside tour of the inner workings of our brain.

What's important to take from this section is that what has happened to you, what was done to you, was not your fault. How your brain reacted and how you have continued to react is not your fault and is outside of your control.

It is, however, within your control to do the work necessary to help you heal and be more aware of your own attachment style in your relationships and how that affects said relationships so you can bring about positive change.[17]

Attachment-Related Trauma

** Trigger warning for mentions of abuse, child abuse, sexual trauma, childhood trauma.**

Attachment trauma is quite simply any kind of event or circumstance that prevents an attachment or bonding process from taking place between an infant and a parent or primary caregiver.

Trauma, by definition, is an event or experience that causes you to feel like your life is potentially in jeopardy. It serves as a great shock to the nervous system (which includes your brain) and can cause lasting damage when you're exposed to recurring traumatic experiences over time. This usually results in being diagnosed with a condition called C-PTSD or Complex-PTSD, which is similar to, but also different from PTSD (Post-Traumatic Stress Disorder).

So, attachment trauma relates more to consistent feelings of being unsafe in your home environment as a child. This may be due to certain abusive family dynamics like substance abuse, poverty, domestic abuse, a sudden change like losing a parent, etc.

Trauma is not so much about what happens to you but what happens inside of you, inside of your nervous system and how that causes you to think and feel certain things—and how that goes on to affect how you function later on as an adult in various scenarios. It's an insidious concept that is misunderstood by many.

Attachment trauma can also take place when a parent or primary caregiver is a source of distress to a child rather than a haven of safety as they should be. For example, a parent who constantly shouts at a baby for crying instead of picking them up and comforting them. Or a parent who sexually abuses or beats a child on a regular basis. It could also be a result of a primary caregiver who completely ignores their child's needs, like leaving a baby to cry for hours on end without comforting them or ignoring their child who seeks emotional comfort after having hurt themselves, etc.

Attachment trauma doesn't only manifest emotionally, but physically as well, as it triggers your nervous system. Responses like anxiety or panic are prime examples of this. These are things you experience physically in the present as a result of something you experienced emotionally in the past. Let's say a child's father has a habit of coming home drunk on Friday evenings and physically abusing the child by beating them without rhyme or reason. What do you think will happen the third or fourth Friday evening before the child's father arrives home? That child's nervous system will be in complete fight or flight mode as they anxiously await their fate, causing them to shake, maybe feel nauseous, panic, etc.

More covert causes of attachment trauma may include:

✧ A parent who is emotionally unavailable to their child.

✧ A controlling and overpowering parent who takes away their child's individuality.

✧ Unprocessed trauma passed on from parent to child without them realizing. Generational trauma can be quite prevalent.

✧ A parent or primary caregiver who objectifies a child's body.

✧ Treatment that causes a child to take on the role of an adult, as in the case of having personal boundaries and sharing adult issues with a child, making them feel like they are now responsible for taking on these issues.

✧ A parent or primary caregiver who suffers from a mental illness that causes them to be less capable of and less available to look after the child.

✧ Using psychological tactics to torture, punish, or control a child.[18]

Just as with any other type of trauma, attachment trauma also plays a significant role in predicting what someone might struggle with later in life.

Attachment Across the Lifespan

When contemplating the consequences of trauma across one's lifespan, we need to look at factors that contribute to stability and change.

What's really exciting to know is that research exists that has focused on how children who are adopted from previously abusive environments at a young age are able to adapt and change their attachment style in response to a new environment. This depends on a stable and loving new environment, of course.

Variables like greater emotional openness, fewer negative life events, and relationship satisfaction have been shown to play a role in changing attachment from insecure to secure.

A child's brain develops at a rapid rate from the moment it starts growing in its mother's womb. Once born, this development continues until the child reaches age 25. Between the moment you're born and age 25, your brain is not yet fully developed. It always fascinates me when adults expect children to have the abilities of adulthood, like fully developed emotional reasoning and critical thinking skills.

The positive side to this is that a child's brain can handle change far better than an adult brain. We now know that the brain is plastic, and that we can learn new things and change certain structures in the brain until the day we die. However, in childhood, the neural connections that form to create certain behaviors do so much faster than in adulthood. This is why it's much easier to learn a new language or to play an instrument in childhood than in adulthood. In the same manner, if a child who comes from an insecure, unsafe home environment is adopted into a secure, supportive, and loving environment, they still have a chance at recovery and adopting a more secure attachment style.

However, when a child who comes from a previously secure home environment is suddenly adopted into an insecure home environment, the change that takes effect may be even stronger and longer lasting.

It is easier to break something that is whole than to fix something that has been smashed into pieces.

There also exists a great deal of research and support for intergenerational transmission of attachment styles. "That's how I was brought up, and I turned out fine." Sound familiar? It's this acceptance of what you have been taught to be gospel and a lack of critical inquiry that leads to perpetuating intergenerational trauma and insecure attachment styles. Unless an individual practices enough self-awareness to realize that there were things in their past that caused them harm in one way or another and that they want to do things differently when they have children of their own.

People who are known as "cycle breakers" often choose not to have any children of their own as a way of making sure that there is no chance that the toxic intergenerational cycle can continue.

Either way, there is simply no denying that the experiences we are exposed to in childhood can have a lasting effect on us for the rest of our lives, and that they do so more often than not.[19]

Attachment and Emotional Regulation

These are key elements that are not discussed enough in various settings. Your ability (or lack thereof) to regulate your own emotions has an enormous impact on the quality of your life. Sadly, so few of us were ever taught how to regulate what can sometimes be overwhelmingly big emotions. Especially for a child.

As adults, we tend to forget what it felt like to struggle with big emotions as a child. So, we often become irritated when a child doesn't know how to regulate themselves. It is extremely unfair to expect a child to know how to do this if no one's ever cared enough to teach them. Then there's also the case where the child's parent was never taught, or if they never took the time to teach themselves (as a result of a lack of awareness or otherwise) how to regulate their *own* emotions and therefore are either not aware of, or do not know, how to teach this vital skill to their child.

Early attachment strongly influences our ability to learn how to regulate ourselves in both pleasant and unpleasant situations and how we learn to communicate our feelings and our needs. Emotional regulation relates to how we experience and express our emotions and is a very important regulator in all our relationships. Emotional regulation skills and the quality of a child's attachment formation are very closely linked to one another. When a child develops an insecure attachment, it leads to feelings of being overwhelmed and unsafe. This, in turn, can lead to either hyperarousal (feeling on edge or highly alert) or hypoarousal (feeling numb inside), which, if left unaddressed, can stay with you throughout your life and have an enormous impact on the quality of your relationships, romantic or otherwise.[20]

When someone is not able to regulate their own emotions, it often leads to them seeking comfort in other ways. When you are feeling overwhelmed or on edge, those emotions need an out somehow. Without the necessary guidance, an individual may choose to find a sense of relief in substances, food, sex, aggression, picking fights, self-harm behaviors like cutting or attempting suicide or simply shutting down.

People who suffer from personality or mood disorders often also struggle with emotional regulation skills due to the intense emotions that they experience. So, it makes sense then, that many children who show anxious attachment in childhood, without there being any negative or inconsistent parenting elements in their environment, often go on to be diagnosed with Borderline Personality Disorder or a mood disorder like Major Depressive Disorder.

How to Practice Emotional Regulation Effectively

There are various tools and strategies available that can help you learn how to regulate your own emotions more effectively. Learning how to regulate your inner world can have a vastly positive effect on your life, ranging from your sense of self-worth to the quality of your relationships. Imagine no longer being a slave to your emotions. No longer having automatic knee-jerk reactions when certain people or situations trigger negative emotions within you that lead to verbal explosions that you never meant to happen but couldn't control.

Learning how to regulate your own emotions is one of the most self-empowering things you can gift yourself. As an added bonus, it also teaches you how to be more mindful of your thoughts and thinking processes. It's a win-win all round.

The tools I'd like to share with you here are rooted in DBT or Dialectical Behavior Therapy. It is a psychological framework and a type of CBT (Cognitive Behavioral Therapy) that was specifically designed to help those who struggle with intense emotions by American psychologist Marsha Linehan in the 1970s.[21]

Here are 3 tools for you to practice becoming more aware of, and better regulate, your own emotions.

1. In the moment

For this exercise you are going to bring your focus to this moment here and now. We want to focus on calming your nervous system so it can back down to a level where you are more in control. Your nervous system is reactive when overwhelmed because it feels unsafe (the nervous system consists of your brain, spinal cord and nerves throughout the body). So, you want to engage in activities that will signal that you are indeed safe and can relax. Remember, it's trying to protect you. Its learned behavior is just, unfortunately, still based on out-of-date data.

If you want to communicate with your nervous system, the best way is to do it through sensation and movement. There are a few things you can try to soothe your nervous system:

- ❖ **Take a cold shower:** The sudden change in temperature helps "shock" your nervous system out of that fight or flight response. With the growing popularity of cold showers or cold plunges, some studies are now showing a potential increase in dopamine when exposing yourself to cold water for a few minutes (really cold, like ice cold). This release of dopamine helps elevate your mood and gives you a sense of calm.

- ❖ **Hold an ice cube:** This is something I've done before when I've felt overwhelmingly anxious and didn't have a shower available (like at the office). The cold temperature of the ice cube gives your mind something else to focus on. Running the ice cube against your neck and holding it to your head can potentially help lower your heart rate. This is essentially a mindfulness exercise.[22]

✧ **Listen to music**: What a beautiful gift music is to humanity. Music can evoke all kinds of emotions, so listening to happy, uplifting, or calm music when you're feeling overwhelmed can also help bring down your heart rate, give your mind something else to focus on, and help your nervous system calm down.

2. Opposite Action to Emotion

This one can feel a bit strange to begin with, but it becomes more effective the more you practice it. Just as with anything else in life.

This is a great technique for helping to deal with and change particularly painful emotions. The premise of this technique is that you can help alleviate the overwhelm that you experience caused by certain emotions by setting in motion an action that is helpful rather than hurtful.

Instead of reacting to feelings of anger, a more helpful response would be to do the opposite of what you feel like doing. So, walking away instead of engaging in an argument. Or listening to uplifting music instead of getting in a fight. Watching funny cat videos on YouTube instead of bashing your fist against a wall.

This way, you are channeling your energy into something more positive and productive. Over time, it will also bring about permanent behavioral change. The key is to stick with it, though.

3. Check the Facts!

We so often tend to misinterpret a situation, which can cause a whole host of problems, including emotional dysregulation that can negatively influence a relationship. This is why it's always important to take a step back at the moment to check the facts before you respond.

For example, Allison's boss, who didn't greet her when she arrived at the office, caused Allison to feel upset, confused, and let down. Because she jumped to a conclusion and decided that her boss was upset with her, it caused her to have this negative emotional response. She might go on to ignore her boss during the day or behave in a passive-aggressive manner. How do you think her boss may interpret that? How do you think it may impact their relationship?

Instead, Allison could have taken a moment to go and ask her boss if everything was okay and if she had heard her when she had greeted her this morning. She may find that her boss didn't hear her, and her not greeting Allison back was not an act of aggression or derision at all.

Case solved. No need for negative emotions.[23]

Now, Allison may feel ashamed or embarrassed. In this instance, it's important for you to remember that there is no place for judgment or self-flagellation on this journey. Only self-compassion. We all make mistakes. The key is to view it as a learning opportunity. Learn from it and move on.

Effective emotional regulation, as with any other skill related to personal development and our relationships, is all based on your level of self-awareness. The more we turn our daily focus to becoming more self-aware of the thoughts we have, the emotions we experience, and how these affect our behavioral responses, the better we'll be able to practice the pause (which means catching yourself in that moment when you feel overwhelmed and just pausing to take a step back and evaluate the situation instead of giving in to a knee-jerk reaction that could land you in trouble or worsen the situation) to think about what is going on inside of us at that very moment and what the best way to respond or move forward would be.

In the next chapter, I'll help you identify your specific attachment style and understand trauma and neglect in childhood and how that may have contributed to things you struggle with today, as well as helpful exercises to help you take control of intrusive thoughts and overwhelming emotions.

Chapter 4

Breaking Chains

"Happy is the person who has broken the chains which hurt the mind."

Ovid

This is where we really start getting into identifying and understanding your specific style of attachment and where it may stem from. We've already gone over the different attachment styles and unpacked anxious attachment. I want us to explore the other insecure attachment styles as well, so you have a more informed understanding of all the attachment styles not associated with secure attachment.

Identifying Other Insecure Attachment Styles

An insecure attachment is one that develops due to any lack of trust or a lack of a secure foundational base. The anxious, avoidant, and disorganized attachment styles would all qualify as insecure attachments. An insecure attachment style has a significant impact on how we approach our relationships. In a secure attachment, you are able to enter a relationship with trust and optimism. But someone with an insecure attachment style will enter a relationship filled with fear and uncertainty, constantly on the lookout for any signs of danger, whether it be physical, psychological, or emotional danger.

You already know that there are four different types of attachment styles and that three of those fall under what would be referred to as insecure, namely:

✧ Anxious attachment.

✧ Avoidant attachment.

✧ Disorganized attachment.

We've covered anxious attachment style, so in this section, I'd like for us to focus a bit more on the other insecure attachment styles and how they may manifest in adulthood, especially as they relate to your romantic relationships. Other relationships like the ones you have with your friends and family are important as well, of course, but it is usually our romantic attachments that have the greatest potential for inflicting deeper emotional and psychological wounds than some of our other relationships. Let's take a look at how avoidant and disorganized attachment styles may emerge in a romantic relationship.

Avoidant Attachment

Glenn isn't someone who has ever been particularly interested in any kind of romantic involvement. He enjoys his independence and has never really seen the point of needing a romantic partner. He's always been most content when doing life on his own. Other people generally tend to see him as someone who comes across as cold, distant, and disinterested in others.

Glenn has a particular love for the game of chess, and despite all the aforementioned, he met someone at a coffee shop not too far from where he lives, where people come to have coffee and play chess against other game enthusiasts. To his surprise, he found that he quite liked this individual and asked if they wanted to meet again for coffee and chess the next week.

This became an institution between the two of them. Every week, at the same time, they would meet at the coffee shop for a cuppa joe and play chess. They had gotten to know one another a little better through the conversations that they'd had. However, whenever probed for more intimate details of himself, Glenn would always seem to clam up or change the subject.

This other individual thought that perhaps he was just one of those cerebral types who are generally regarded as socially awkward and less emotionally intelligent. However, when they plucked up enough courage to ask him out to dinner one day, Glenn became obviously uncomfortable and just said "no" quite bluntly before leaving without any further explanation.

That was the end of their weekly coffee and chess meet-ups.

Were you able to identify some clues in this story that are indicative of someone who has an avoidant attachment style as compared to the information we covered in Chapter 1? Let's look at some signs of avoidant attachment again:

✧ Prefer to be alone when upset.

✧ Uncomfortable with being touched or any other form of intimacy.

✧ They are not good at accepting any kind of criticism.

✧ Can seem quite cold and don't like to show emotions.

✧ They avoid getting too close to others. So, they have very few, if any, friends.

✧ They are fearful of commitment, so they avoid it altogether.

✧ They prefer to be alone or independent and don't easily invest in any type of close relationship.[24]

Now, let's have a look at Glenn's history.

He grew up with only his mother, who became a single parent after his abusive father up and left them one day when Glenn was only 3 years old. His mother struggled on her own. She worked two different jobs to cover the essentials. Glenn was left with their next-door neighbor during the day, who was also a single lady but quite a bit older than his mother. This lady only did it for the bit of money that Glenn's mother could afford to pay her.

During the day, she would ignore Glenn and leave him to cry for hours on end when he needed something. Whether it was out of hunger or maybe having fallen and hurt himself. And, by the time his mother came to fetch him at night after work, she was too tired to give him any attention either and would feel overwhelmed by his crying, shouting at him to stop. He spent most of his childhood borderline malnourished and completely neglected emotionally and psychologically.

Let's compare this with what we know about the possible causes of an avoidant attachment style:

- ⬧ Ignoring a child when they cry or show any signs of distress or fear.
- ⬧ Suppressing a child's display of emotion when they're crying by telling them to stop or shut up.
- ⬧ Shaming a child for showing emotion. E.g., *"You're such a crybaby."*
- ⬧ Having unrealistic expectations in terms of a child's ability to look after themselves. Like expecting Glenn to be able to look after his own needs at 5 years of age.[25]

Combining the causes of an avoidant attachment style, along with the symptoms that usually present themselves in relationships in adulthood, it's clear to see that Glenn suffers from an avoidant attachment style and why. The question is: can someone with this type of insecure attachment style heal in a way that would help them adopt a more secure attachment style? The very promising answer is, yes, it is possible. With the help of therapy and ongoing personal work, it is absolutely possible. It just takes time. So, if you are in a relationship with someone with this type of attachment style, patience, empathy, and compassion are needed.

Disorganized Attachment

Jada is a beautiful, unencumbered woman in her mid-thirties. A strong, proud black woman with a degree in corporate management and a thriving career with one of the largest companies in corporate America. She sounds like someone who has it together, doesn't she? Sometimes, she does. However, for the most part, she swings between tumultuous, abusive relationships and borderline self-isolation. She never sees herself as the beautiful, successful woman she is and tends to be extremely self-critical.

Deep down, Jada really does have a need for someone who will show her love and kindness. Someone who would care enough to want to get to know and understand her. On the other hand, she runs when a relationship gets too serious, fearful of getting trapped or hurt.

There are times when she allows herself to open up just to engage in a surface-like, more-sexual-than-anything-else relationship. However, the moment she allows herself to have even the slightest feelings for someone else, she turns into a clingy, needy person that she loathes. She fears her partner will see her as someone who can't handle or take care of herself and leave.

She's had so many bad relationships that she figures it would be better to invest all her energy in her career and do life on her own. That way, there's no way for her to get hurt and she can do absolutely whatever she wants.

Okay, let's compare Jada's story with the possible causes of a disorganized attachment style:

- ✧ Struggles with vulnerability.

- ✧ Low self-esteem.

- ✧ A struggle to deal with intense emotions.

- ✧ Inconsistencies in relationships.

- ✧ Depression.

- ✧ Avoiding relationships.

- ✧ Getting anxious or fearful when someone gets too close emotionally.

- ✧ Fear of abandonment.

Jada comes from a broken home. Her parents divorced when she was still a baby, and since then, she lived her entire life between two houses until she finished college and managed to move into a place of her own.

Jada's mom is warm and caring, but a mean drunk. Her father is a strict disciplinarian, but a kind man who dotes on his daughter.

Jada's mom started having problems with alcohol when Jada was about eight years old. Whenever it was her mom's turn to have her for the week, Jada would come home to a house that looked like someone had broken in and turned everything over. Her mom would be passed out drunk on the couch in the middle of the day. By the time she finally woke up, it would be around dinner time, and she'd be yelling at Jada to make her some food. She'd verbally abuse her daughter all the time, telling her that she'd never amount to anything in life. But then there would be times when she would be clean, sober, and the kindest woman on the planet. She'd be affectionate with Jada and ensure she had everything she needed.

At her dad's place, she received the structure and care she needed from a parent. Although strict, Jada's father always treated her with respect and kindness, ensuring she was well cared for. However, if she ever did anything that her father deemed unacceptable, he would beat her with anything within reach at the time. Whether it be a belt or a baseball bat, you name it.

What do we know about the potential causes of a disorganized attachment style?

✧ This attachment style is usually caused by unpredictable parenting that confuses a child and causes them to feel fearful. Feelings of uncertainty and fear are central to the cause of this type of attachment style. There's no consistency. The child never really knows what's going to happen next. Hence, "disorganized."[26]

Some common threads run through the insecure attachment styles. Like the fear of abandonment and being vulnerable with someone else. It stems from lessons learned early on in life that vulnerability potentially equals pain. And, once someone loves you, they will eventually hurt you and leave you. Because that's what a child learned from the adults around them. It's what we call childhood trauma.

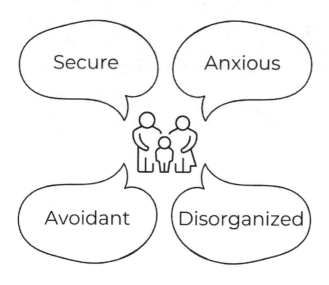

Childhood Trauma and Neglect

I often hear someone say, *"What I went through wasn't traumatic like some of the stories you hear online of a child having been locked up in a cage.* **The reality is that trauma is a topic that is grossly misunderstood by the majority of people in two different ways.**

The first is where someone might use the term trauma in a trivializing manner, for example, *"I had to stand in a queue to get tickets for over an hour. I'm so traumatized."*

The second is where someone overlooks their own experience of trauma because they feel it doesn't fall within the category of being grave enough to qualify as trauma.

Let's qualify the term here to clear up any confusion. The term *trauma* refers to a deeply distressing emotional response to an event. Many different events *can* qualify as traumatic, for example:

⬧ Living with parents who are addicts.

⬧ Being involved in a car accident.

- ✧ Being diagnosed with a terminal illness.
- ✧ Watching someone else get shot or stabbed or hurt in some manner.
- ✧ Being forced to do something you do not want to, which makes you feel unsafe emotionally, like in the case of sexual abuse.
- ✧ Breaking a limb.
- ✧ Being a victim of a crime or witnessing a crime.
- ✧ Being constantly put down, ignored, shouted at, or belittled, etc.
- ✧ Any form of emotional or psychological abuse.

In children, any event that evokes a feeling of intense fear for their safety or their life is considered a traumatic event. These events are usually violent, dangerous, or life-threatening. However, emotional and psychological neglect or torture also qualify as trauma.

So you see, many different types of experiences can qualify as traumatic. However, having to stand in a queue for hours to get tickets to a Taylor Swift concert does not qualify as traumatic, nor should one trivialize such an important matter.

The effects of emotional neglect in children can be incredibly subtle. It's important to understand that not all emotional neglect equates to emotional abuse. It's often not done intentionally. For instance, let's say a little girl comes to her mother seemingly upset, telling her that a certain child is being mean to her at school, and her mom sees it as normal obstacles we all face in childhood and brushes her off. It's not that she intentionally ignored her child's need for comfort and support. But, over time, these interactions teach the child that their emotions and needs are unimportant.

Abuse is **always** intentional. So when it comes to any child having been exposed to any kind of abuse in childhood, you can know that it was done with that person knowing what they were doing, knowing that it was wrong, and doing it anyway. There are many reasons why some adults abuse children. That's a whole other book.

Children are resilient. But they're also emotionally sensitive and vulnerable in their early developmental years. When they experience consistent ACEs, or Adverse Childhood Experiences, it causes them to form certain negative beliefs about themselves and the world around them, as well as carrying wounds within them that sometimes never get resolved.

Along with attachment styles, a condition that greatly affects children who have experienced multiple ACEs in early childhood is C-PTSD. Complex PTSD is a trauma-related psychiatric condition similar to PTSD but with far more nuance and complexity. A child who grows up to be an adult who gets diagnosed with C-PTSD might struggle with many of the same things that individuals with insecure attachment struggle with, like:

- ✧ A fear of abandonment.
- ✧ Low self-esteem.
- ✧ Feeling worthless.
- ✧ Finding it difficult to connect with others.
- ✧ Fear of vulnerability.
- ✧ Suicidal tendencies.
- ✧ Substance abuse.
- ✧ Anxiety.
- ✧ Depression.
- ✧ Emotional dysregulation.
- ✧ Hypervigilance.
- ✧ Intrusive negative thoughts.
- ✧ Struggles with sleep and having nightmares.

✧ Experiencing flashbacks.

✧ Difficulty forming and maintaining close relationships.[27]

If you have been diagnosed with or suspect yourself of suffering from C-PTSD, see the resources guide at the back of the book for useful links that will help you better understand the condition and treatment options.

Dysfunctional Family Dynamics

I don't think I've ever known anyone who hasn't at least joked about their family being dysfunctional. True dysfunction is not a joking matter for those who have had to live through and deal with the sometimes severe consequences that follow.

What makes a family dysfunctional

Dysfunction within a family can be quite nuanced. One might think it would be obvious from the outside, but it is rarely the case. It can be quite challenging to explain what exactly makes a family dynamic dysfunctional or normal. "*Normal*" is a relative term that can differ from one person to the next.

Obvious signs of dysfunction might be things like:

✧ Excessive criticism.

✧ A lack of unconditional love.

✧ Addiction.

✧ A lack of communication.

✧ Gaslighting.

✧ Abuse.

✧ An unpredictable environment.

✧ Lack of intimacy.

✧ Emotional dysregulation.

✧ Lack of boundaries.

✧ Lack of empathy.

✧ Excessively strict rules.

✧ Isolation.

✧ Fear.

✧ Loneliness.

✧ Controlling behavior.

✧ Codependence.

✧ Perfectionism.[28]

There are so many possible signs. What's most important is the impact that the dysfunction has had on you. How has it affected your quality of life, your self-esteem, your relationships, etc.?

That being said, there are specific patterns in dysfunctional families that are fairly easily identifiable.

Triangulation: This is where two family members gang up against another individual in the family. Like an abusive father using his child to team up against the mother/wife by telling the child stories about how bad their mother is. A classic example of triangulation would be what you see in a divorce where a child is involved and carries messages between parents, chooses sides, and distracts their parents to avoid conflict.

Gaslighting: This is especially prevalent in families where there is at least one narcissistic parent. Gaslighting is a psychological tactic used to make you question your own sanity or grip on reality. For example, when you confront someone for having said something hurtful to you, and they point blank deny ever having said it. They might say something like, *"Are you losing it or just* *making stuff up now? I swear I never said it.*" Or they may say something like, "*Maybe that's what you remember, but it's certainly not how I remember it.*"

Stonewalling: Another classic psychological tactic where someone will refuse to engage with another until they succumb to their demands. It could be that they feel the other person offended them, and now they're refusing to engage with them until they've apologized. Or, perhaps, they want another family member to admit that they did something wrong and refuse to engage until they do so. It can make it very difficult to move forward and is often the type of behavior that causes another to form a fear of abandonment because someone who tends to use stonewalling as a tactic will also very likely make use of threats to go with it.

The biggest problem in dysfunctional families is that no one knows or has ever been taught how to communicate and regulate their own emotions effectively. In some cases, there may be an element of mental illness in a family. However, depending on the type of illness, most people would have the ability to learn how to regulate their own emotions, at least to a level where it is not harmful to others.

Addiction is another major issue facing millions of families worldwide. When one or both parents suffer from addiction, they do not have the capacity or awareness to tend to a child's needs.

And, as I have shared a number of times, when a child feels unheard or unimportant, it causes them to believe that they are unimportant and not worthy of being heard, loved, or attended to.

Children often have to neglect their own feelings so they can tune in to the feelings of those around them to survive or make themselves feel safe. For example, a child might learn that when their father's voice takes on a certain tone, it means trouble, and they need to hide; otherwise, they'll get caught in the path of his rage. Another might learn that consoling their mother after their parents have fought will earn their mother's attention. So, they are so attuned to the emotions of everyone around them, they fall completely out of touch with their own. And, if you never have a role model who was secure enough to teach you the skills needed to be aware of and to take care of your own emotions and needs, the development of these incredibly important skills becomes stunted.

A child is like a sponge. I'm sure you've heard this saying before. They absorb everything that goes on around them and tend to notice things that they miss in adulthood. Subtle behaviors in a parent's body language tell them whether they are safe or not. Someone's tone of voice signals the child's nervous system of potential imminent danger.

Even so, a child doesn't have the processing capabilities or cognitive functioning that an adult has yet. Obviously, they don't. It takes 25 years for a brain to reach full maturity. It is baffling how some adults often expect a child to understand something that is obviously well beyond their years.[29]

The good news is that over the years, as more and more research into child development and the after-effects of adverse experiences in childhood have been investigated, more tools are available to help you start the healing process today than ever before.

Somatic Exercises for Healing

The word "somatic" means "related to the physical body." So, related to the body as opposed to the mind.

When it comes to having an insecure attachment style, whether it be anxious, avoidant, or disorganized, there's bound to be a level of anxiety and dysregulation that goes with it. When you go through childhood, exposure to multiple adverse experiences teaches your brain and body certain things. It teaches it to always be on the lookout and vigilant of any kind of danger, whether real or perceived. Emotional and psychological wounds experienced in your formative years also remain within your body, whether you're aware of it or not. Your body remembers trauma and carries it, perhaps for your entire life, unless you become aware of and learn how to heal from it.

Trauma can make you physically sick. It can be held in the body for years and lead to all sorts of illnesses later on in life, like anxiety, chronic pain, headaches, hypervigilance, depression, and so much more.[30] Every time we are faced with triggers in the present, it just further perpetuates the symptoms associated with the illnesses we struggle with as a result of abuse and trauma from the past.

In this section, we'll cover a number of somatic exercises you can use to help release the stress, pain, tension, and wounds still present in the body so it can help you heal on a physical as well as an emotional level.

1. The Body Scan

This technique is seen as an active meditation exercise that can help you relax and become more aware of what's going on in your body. How often do we pause to take stock of what our bodies need? That pain in your hip that's always present. Do you ignore it or tend to it? When you ignore it, what are you telling your body? That it's not worth tending to, perhaps?

The body scan is designed to achieve a number of things. It helps you relax, practice mindfulness, practice meditation, and become more aware of different sensations in your body.

Here's how it works:

- ✧ Find somewhere where you can sit quietly and not be disturbed.

- ✧ Find a comfortable position to sit in. This can be in a chair or on the floor; it doesn't matter. Then close your eyes and take a few deep breaths in and out.

- ✧ Now, bring your focus to your lower body. Your feet, your calves, your knees, your thighs, hamstrings, hips, and pelvis. Linger in this area and become aware of these body parts of yours. Can you identify any pressure, tension, tightness, or warmth? Any aches or pains?

- ✧ When you notice any tension or pain in a certain part of your body, take a deep breath in and then focus on completely relaxing that body part as you exhale, releasing any pain or discomfort.

- ✧ When you're done scanning your lower body, do the same for your upper body and also include some of your major organs. Like your intestines, heart, lungs, brain, etc.

- ✧ When you are done scanning your entire body, just sit for a moment and practice breathing in deeply through your nose, all the way into your tummy, then slowly exhaling through your mouth. Do this ten times, then slowly open your eyes.

Notice how you feel after having done this exercise? Do you feel more relaxed? Did you notice anything that needed attention while you were doing the body scan? Maybe you noticed that you actually feel a bit dehydrated and need to drink more water. Or perhaps you realized your hips are really tight, and you need to incorporate more stretching exercises into your daily routine. This exercise helps you to check in with and take care of your body, so it knows that it is loved and worthy of good health.

2. The Butterfly Hug

This is an exercise that falls under a therapeutic framework called EMDR, which stands for Eye Movement Desensitization and Reprocessing. It is a therapeutic framework that has gained a lot of attention in recent years for its seeming efficacy in helping treat symptoms of PTSD and C-PTSD. It used bilateral (opposite sides) stimulation in combination with reprocessing painful memories from the past. Although we don't know exactly why it works, the process of activating both hemispheres of the brain through bilateral stimulation so various regions of the brain are activated in combination with your nervous system. This has been shown to reduce the vividness of emotions associated with trauma.[31]

The butterfly hug is a very simple yet powerful self-soothing exercise for grounding yourself and dealing with overwhelming emotions. Here's how it works:

✧ Find a quiet place where you won't be interrupted, and sit up tall with your back straight, either on a chair, couch, or on the floor.

✧ Close your eyes and practice deep breathing, in through your nose and out through your mouth.

✧ Notice any emotions that come up as you're doing this exercise, and just breathe through it.

✧ Cross your hands over your chest, interlocking your thumbs and resting each middle finger on your collarbone. Fan out your fingers, relaxing your hands.

✧ It's this interlocking of the thumbs and fingers fanned that makes it look like a butterfly, hence the name.

✧ Now, you're going to alternate tapping each side with your middle fingers (left, right, left, right, etc.) for eight to ten rounds.

✧ Stop between each round to practice awareness surrounding your emotions and distress level. Then do another round. Repeat for five rounds.

Some people find this exercise quite cathartic as they experience a sudden rush and release of emotions. Some people cry. Others simply enjoy the feeling of the "hug." There is no right or wrong thing to feel. You're simply observing and practicing being aware of your body's response. Notice how you feel when you've completed the exercise. A good idea I always recommend is to journal about your experiences with these exercises so you can keep track of your progress.

3. Grounding Exercises

These are great for bringing your attention to the here and now instead of being overwhelmed by memories from the past or worrying about something that might or might not happen in the future. There are many different grounding exercises for you to try out. Here are a few of my favorites.

- ✧ **Holding an ice cube.** What this does is help bring your attention to the block of ice because it's a significant change in your environment. Your brain immediately focuses on it because it's cold. Really cold. You can also run the ice over your wrists and neck. The cold temperature helps lower your blood pressure, which helps lower any levels of anxiety you might be experiencing.

- ✧ **Move your body.** The main idea of this exercise is to move your body in a way that feels comfortable to you. Stretching, yoga, Pilates, and dancing are all prime examples of activities you can choose for this exercise. Focus on becoming aware of every body part as you move. What does your body feel like? Tune in to your muscles contracting and relaxing, your lungs taking in air to feed your body with oxygen. Notice how your joints feel, etc. This is a great way of connecting and getting in tune with your body while practicing mindfulness and becoming more aware of your body's needs.[33]

Any exercise that presents you with the opportunity to connect with and become more aware of your body can be considered a somatic exercise. When combined with therapy, it can be a powerful tool for healing.

Embracing Mindfulness and Visualization

Visualization and mindfulness exercises are excellent for teaching yourself how to regulate your thoughts and your emotions while also lessening symptoms associated with trauma. Here are some great ones to get you started.

Mindfulness Meditation - Thoughts are Clouds

This is one of my favorite mindfulness meditation exercises. People often mistakenly believe that meditation is all about clearing the mind and trying not to think of anything at all. If you try to do this, I can guarantee you will fail. It is impossible to shut down your brain and not have any thoughts unless you are dead.

The idea of this exercise is to learn how to simply observe your thoughts with compassion and then allow them to float away like clouds. We too often judge ourselves for not being able to clear our minds during an exercise like this. Your thoughts are just thoughts; you don't need to judge them as anything else.

How to do this exercise:

✧ Find a place where you can sit or lie down comfortably and won't be disturbed for at least ten to fifteen minutes. Sitting is better otherwise you might doze off like I tend to.

✧ Close your eyes and practice some deep breathing for ten counts.

Deep breath in through your nose, all the way into your belly, and out through your mouth.

✧ Now, just keep focusing on your breathing. Use the words "in" and "out" as a simple mantra as you breathe in and out. In and out, in and out.

✧ Soon, you'll notice random thoughts popping up. Don't get frustrated. Remember, they're just thoughts. Simply acknowledge the thought, then visualize it floating away like a cloud and bring your attention back to your breathing, in and out, in and out.

✧ Do this for ten minutes, then slowly open your eyes and gently stretch out your body.

How did you find the exercise? Did you feel frustrated when thoughts kept popping up in your mind? Did you struggle to bring your focus back to your breathing at times? This is normal. It takes practice, and with every session, you'll get better at developing your ability to see thoughts for what they are—just thoughts. How does this help in your everyday life? Well, it translates into you being able to take a moment when an intrusive or negative thought pops into your mind. This is an excellent way of becoming more aware of your thinking patterns, which will come in handy when it comes to changing them to serve you in a more positive, healthier way.

Mindfulness Visualization - The Sahara

This exercise is similar to the one above, but instead of visualizing your thoughts as clouds, you're going to visualize yourself in the Sahara Desert. When a thought pops into your mind, see it displayed on the dunes as if through a projector. Then, imagine a gust of wind wiping that thought away, leaving only sand behind. Then you'll turn your focus back to your breathing, just as you did with the Thoughts are Clouds exercise.

Mindfulness and visualization exercises are excellent tools you can use to help you whenever you are feeling anxious or overwhelmed. They teach you how to become more self-aware and let go of what we all tend to hold onto that's not good for us, like stress and obsessive negative thoughts. I suggest you try out all the exercises in this book and find what works best for you. Then, focus on building a daily habit of including these exercises in your routine. Maybe first thing in the morning after you've woken up or before you go to bed. Or both. It will help set up your day and provide a good way to wind down. It helps you build resilience in the moment so you can move forward.

Building Self-Compassion

No one is as hard on us as we are on ourselves. Especially when you've grown up in an environment where you were always kept to unrealistic expectations, where you had to be perfect in order to avoid some form of abuse or compete for someone's love and adoration by being something other than yourself. Self-compassion is your ability to treat yourself with kindness and not constantly judge yourself for mistakes or perceived flaws.

It is a crucial part of the healing process because if you cannot treat yourself with love and compassion, you might always seek it in places where you might get hurt even further.

Studies have shown that fostering self-compassion helps to diminish negative self-talk, self-criticism, and judgment of self. It reduces stress levels, which means it also lowers cortisol levels, which is the stress hormone responsible for various stress-related illnesses when there's too much of it in the body. It also showed that self-compassion practices encourage more secure attachment in one's relationships.[34]

It may take some time and effort to get used to being kind to yourself when all you've ever known is insecurity. But turning acceptance, understanding, love, and kindness inwards means you are able to provide for yourself what others have neglected to in the past.

It's also important for healing feelings of shame. Abuse, trauma, insecure childhood environments, whatever you'd like to call it, often cause a child to feel like they must have done something wrong to have deserved the treatment they received in childhood. Feelings of shame very often go hand-in-hand with insecure attachment. Practicing self-compassion helps you start the process of forgiving yourself for thinking that you didn't deserve love, kindness, understanding, etc.

"You cannot give what you do not have." Have you ever heard that saying? You need to have enough love for yourself first to the point that your cup overflows, and whatever overflows is what you can give to others.

How do you practice self-compassion?

- ✧ Being kinder to yourself when you make mistakes or feel frustrated with yourself.
- ✧ Being more patient with yourself.
- ✧ Understanding that you are fallible, as is every other human being on this planet, and that it's normal.
- ✧ Being mindful of your thoughts and emotions when you feel like you are in distress.
- ✧ Doing what you need to look after yourself first.
- ✧ Embracing your flaws as uniquely yours. They are a part of you. And they are as beautiful as every other part of you because they are what makes you human.
- ✧ Letting go of negative thoughts and emotions by engaging in mindfulness and visualization exercises like the ones I've shared with you previously.

- ❖ Being especially kind to yourself when you are struggling, when you are feeling down, or when you feel like you are failing.

- ❖ Treating yourself as you would a friend.

- ❖ Embracing mistakes as opportunities to learn and grow from.

- ❖ Looking at yourself in the mirror and complimenting yourself.

Both anxious and avoidant attachment relate to having difficulties being kind to yourself, along with a propensity for self-judgment. When you are constantly ignored, berated, hurt, vilified, or belittled in your upbringing, it sets the tone for your negative sense of self, which makes it hard to accept and love yourself.

The ability to be kind to yourself and practice self-compassion has been proven to help boost one's mood and overall sense of well-being, as well as your mental health. It also boosts creative thinking, better memory, less illness, and a more positive outlook on life in general.[35]

Secure Attachment: The Goal for Healing

Now that we know what insecure attachment styles look like, the goal is to start implementing the tools and strategies needed that will allow us to move toward adopting a more secure attachment style.

What does secure attachment look like? As we've discovered earlier on, attachment forming has more to do with the nonverbal treatment of a child than any verbal use. It's how you are made to feel that impacts the type of attachment you develop the most.

Your goal now is to start giving yourself the attention, love, support, understanding, kindness, and nurturing that you never received but still crave so deeply. It is more challenging for those of us with insecure attachment styles to implement the steps needed to move toward healing from past experiences, but with compassion and consistency, it is absolutely possible.

In the chapters that follow, we will explore various exercises and techniques that will assist you in healing different aspects of yourself that have been carrying wounds for so many years. We'll explore ways to connect to self and form more secure attachments with others.

Ultimately, I want to share powerful tools with you that will teach you how to take control of your own emotions, set boundaries, advocate for yourself, and effectively communicate your needs.

Onward!

Help Others Discover The Transformative Information in this Book

My mission is to provide content that is not only informative, but also tools that are helpful and practical, as well as easy to implement in everyday life. I ask that you please take a moment to leave a review of this book so other readers like you can find the information they need to transform their lives for the better.

I really appreciate it.

Thank you so much!

Chapter 5

Mindful Moments for Anxious Attachments

"Man is not worried by real problems so much as by his imagined anxieties about real problems."

Epictetus

We continue our journey and will explore even more tools and exercises in this chapter that will help teach you how to tame intrusive, negative, and anxious thoughts that plague you endlessly. It all starts with self-awareness, of course. We can't change something that's not beneficial to us if we're not even aware of it yet. So, let's start there.

Self-Awareness Exercises

When I say self-awareness, I mean it both in general and in terms of practicing compassionate self-awareness. You're essentially reparenting yourself, so there will be times when you need to be stricter with yourself and maintain structure, but there will also be times when you need to practice more kindness, love, and compassion.

The art of self-awareness is all about being curious. Fostering curiosity can come through asking yourself probing questions, pondering the meaning and causes of your actions, and being curious about understanding yourself holistically.

Let's start off with some questions you can ask yourself to gain greater self-awareness:

✧ What dreams or goals do you have for yourself in your life?

✧ Why are these important to you?

✧ What is your greatest strength?

✧ What is your greatest weakness?

✧ What scares you the most in life?

✧ Describe your ideal relationship (romantic relationship)

✧ Do you feel like you treat yourself better than you do others? If not, why?

✧ Do you tend to make decisions logically or intuitively?

✧ What is keeping you from achieving your goals in life?[36]

Take some time to really think about these questions before you answer them. We often answer these types of questions in a way that we feel we won't be judged by others. But no one is here. You're doing this exercise by yourself, so you can answer them honestly.

Other exercises to include are:

✧ **Walking in nature by yourself** and paying attention to your thoughts as you walk along a quiet footpath. The idea with self-awareness is to practice non-judgmental curiosity so you can better examine the problems you face in your life, the causes of these problems and how they affect you, the areas where you may be the cause of your own problems, and what you can do about it.

✧ **Paying attention to your thoughts**. Start a daily journaling exercise. Journaling is an extremely powerful tool for becoming more aware of your thoughts and the different thought patterns you hold. It can help you identify negative or unhelpful thinking so you can do something about changing it. It is a great way of keeping tabs on what is going on inside of your mind.

✧ **Mindfulness meditation exercises.** Like the ones we have covered previously, it can be especially helpful to become more aware of both body and mind. These exercises help you unplug and connect with *"the self"* for greater self-awareness.

Self-awareness is perhaps the most important skill we can develop in our lives. It brings with it a wealth of knowledge about ourselves and the world around us. Knowledge that can help us heal ourselves and practice personal mastery.

I will be sharing more exercises with you throughout this chapter that can aid in gaining greater self-awareness, as well as learning how to regulate yourself in different situations.

Grounding Techniques for Anxiety

With insecure attachment comes symptoms like those associated with hypervigilance that can lead to experiencing symptoms associated with anxiety or panic. Here are some exercises that are helpful for calming your body and mind when you are experiencing anxiety.

The 5-4-3-2-1 Grounding Technique

One of my go-to exercises for whenever I'm experiencing a sudden onset of anxiety. This exercise involves using your senses to help ground yourself in the present moment. It's an exercise you can do anywhere, at any time, and goes like this. Right where you are, focus on and notice:

✧ **5 Things you can see.** Describe them to yourself in your mind by shape, color, and texture.

✧ **4 Things you can touch.** It could be your clothing, pet, phone—anything within reach. Hone in on describing what it feels like to yourself in your mind.

✧ **3 Things you can hear.** Instead of just saying to yourself, "birds," try to describe it in more detail. For example: "The sharp chirping of birds."

✧ **2 Things you can smell.** Smell is one of our strongest senses. Smell your hair (if you have long hair, I wouldn't advise that you randomly smell someone else's hair), hand lotion, coffee, perfume, or anything else you like the smell of.

✧ **1 Thing you can taste.** Again, describe the taste to yourself. Is it bitter, sweet, salty? What's the texture of what you're tasting like?

Using the senses to ground yourself is a great way of calming the nervous system in times of overwhelm.

Count Backward from 100

Even if math is not your strong suit, this is another good exercise to help you ground yourself in the moment. It involves you simply counting backward from 100 by 7. So, 100, 93, 86, 79, etc. It takes effort to focus on doing this exercise, which helps take your mind off everything else that's going on and focus on the task at hand, in the here and now. If counting back from 100 by 7 is too easy, make it more challenging for yourself, e.g., count back from 763 by 13. Whatever makes it challenging enough that it causes you to have to focus.

Listen to Music

Compile a playlist of your favorite music for times like these. Listening to music holds so many health benefits. Putting on a set of headphones or earplugs and just listening to some of your favorite tunes can help tune out the world and bring down levels of anxiety.[37]

The great thing about these types of tools is that you can take them anywhere you go. You can practice them any time you need without anyone knowing you're doing so. The reason I keep repeating this is because, for many people, the thought of others noticing that they're struggling with anxiety already makes them feel even more anxious. So, employing a self-soothing tool that draws even more attention would be counterproductive.

Daily Mindfulness Practices

Here are my top 3 daily mindfulness practices that I work into my daily routine.

Washing Dishes

I know you're asking yourself, *"How can washing dishes be a mindfulness exercise?"* The sensory processing involved in washing dishes makes it a great mindfulness exercise. Think about it: you can focus on the temperature of the water, the smell of the washing liquid, the feel of the sponge or dishcloth in your hand, and the texture of the dishes as you wash them. It's a great way of working mindfulness practices into your day.

Mindful Listening

As the name suggests, this exercise involves you simply tuning in to your sense of hearing and focusing on all the sounds you can hear in your environment. Even better if you can do it outside somewhere, then you can focus on the sound of the bird and any other critters you can hear. If I were doing this exercise right now, I'd hear different birds sounding like they're having an argument outside my office. My cat chattering at the chirping birds. I can hear the keys on my keyboard being hit with every stroke of a finger. I can hear an airplane pass by overhead. I can hear some traffic in the distance. Just writing about what I was hearing helped me feel more grounded and mindful.

People Watching

Something I love doing when in a public space like a mall. In a non-creepy way. I just love observing people and trying to ascertain what they might be thinking or feeling. What kind of person might they be based on what they're wearing? Noticing their facial expressions and the way they walk. There's no judgment involved in this exercise; you're simply observing. When you are focused on noticing others, it gives your brain a break from the incessant internal chatter that goes on inside of your mind all day long.[38]

These are all exercises you can work into your daily routine. People watching can be done at the office as well. It might even help add a sense of mystery as people start to talk among themselves, wondering why you're watching them all of a sudden. I'm kidding.

Self-Regulation Through Breathwork

Using breathing as a way of soothing and grounding yourself in times of distress or when you're feeling anxious or panicked is another fantastic tool to keep in your back pocket.

The relationship between your breathing and your nervous system is an important one. When you are feeling anxious or overwhelmed, you start taking shorter, shallower breaths, breathing faster to get the maximum amount of oxygen in as your fight or flight response gets triggered. So, focusing on taking deep, calm breaths can help counteract this survival mechanism by activating the parasympathetic nervous system and signaling your body that it's safe.

Box Breathing Exercise

The box breathing exercise is great because it's so easy to remember. Here's how it works:

- ✦ Take a deep breath in through your nose for 4 counts.
- ✦ Hold it at the top for 4 counts.
- ✦ Slowly breathe out through your nose for 4 counts.
- ✦ Hold for 4 counts.
- ✦ Repeat 4 times.

If doing it for 4 counts is too easy, you can increase the time to whatever you'd like.

4-7-8 Breathing Exercise

As with the box breathing exercises, the 4-7-8 exercise also involves counting. The difference here is that you want to focus on breathing out for longer than you breathe in. It has been shown that this small detail is important as it helps to activate your parasympathetic nervous system and signal your body to go into the rest and digest state. Here's how it works:

- ✦ Relax your body and sit up straight.
- ✦ Breathe in through your nose for 4 counts.
- ✦ Hold your breath at the top for 7 counts.
- ✦ Then slowly breathe out through your mouth for 8 counts.

You may find that this exercise is more challenging than the box-breathing exercise. Especially when it comes to controlling your breath going out so slowly. If you find it too challenging, reduce the time to 3-5-6 until you're comfortable enough to go back up to the 4-7-8 increments. If it gets too easy, you can adjust by going up to 5-8-9, etc.[39]

When I feel anxiety coming on suddenly, my breathing is the first thing I focus on. Controlling my breathing and slowing it down. Making sure to take deep, controlled breaths in and out through my nose and mouth. It has yet to fail me. Once I feel like I have a bit more control, I then shift my focus to one of the other grounding exercises I've shared here with you, like the 5-4-3-2-1 sensory exercise. But breathing always comes first. Breathing is life. (Have a look at the resources page for more breathing exercises)

Cultivating Emotional Intelligence

Emotional intelligence is the ability to recognize and understand others' emotions and goes hand-in-hand with empathy and compassion. It allows you to recognize that your partner is upset and then respond appropriately, showing them that you care, like telling them that you have noticed they seem upset and asking whether they'd like to talk about it, or if there's anything else you can do to help them feel better.

There are very many different types of intelligence in the world, like:

✦ Cognitive intelligence.

✦ Musical intelligence.

✦ Artistic intelligence.

✦ Linguistic intelligence.

✦ Etc.

Emotional intelligence is what allows us to connect with others in our various relationships. Without it, an intimate relationship with someone else is nearly impossible.

Signs of low emotional intelligence:

- ✧ You tend to hold a grudge.
- ✧ You're quick to make assumptions.
- ✧ You get angry very easily.
- ✧ You cannot regulate your own emotions.
- ✧ You beat yourself up over mistakes you made in the past.
- ✧ You struggle to assert yourself.
- ✧ You tend to blame others for your mistakes, i.e., an inability to take responsibility.
- ✧ You tend to have emotional outbursts.
- ✧ You only ever talk about yourself.
- ✧ You're oblivious to others' feelings.[40]

Signs of high emotional intelligence:

- ✧ Empathy.
- ✧ Being understanding of others' struggles.
- ✧ An ability to effectively communicate your needs.
- ✧ Not taking criticism personally.
- ✧ You know your own strengths and weaknesses.
- ✧ Constantly seeking to improve yourself.
- ✧ You are able to motivate yourself and others.
- ✧ You are not easily offended.
- ✧ You are able to regulate your thoughts, emotions, and behaviors.
- ✧ You lift others up.[41]

How can you cultivate greater emotional intelligence?

1. **Practice observing your emotions** and the cause of these emotions. A great way of doing this is to keep a mood diary. Whenever you become aware of an emotion that you feel and have become aware of, write it down, along with the time of day, location, and what was happening around you at the time.

2. **Practice taking responsibility for your own feelings**: The reality is that no one can MAKE you feel anything at any given time. They might do something that evokes an emotional response within you, but you get to CHOOSE whether you want to engage or step back from the emotion. It takes practice, of course.

3. **Pay others more (sincere) compliments**: This helps you to focus a little less on yourself and do something that makes someone else feel good.

4. **Work together to find solutions:** Instead of shooting others down when it comes to trying to solve a problem, hear others out. Someone might just have a better idea than you.

5. **Engage with people you usually wouldn't**: This can help you gain a perspective on other people's lives, the troubles they face, etc.

6. **Become aware of and acknowledge your emotional triggers**: Ignoring them won't make them go away. Acknowledge your emotional triggers so you can work on healing the parts of you that will help resolve said triggers.

7. **Practice becoming more aware of your thought processes**: This way, you can better identify faulty or negative thoughts that need changing.

8. **Learn to listen more than you talk**: You might learn a thing or two, and it helps you foster greater empathy for others as well.

Working on improving your emotional intelligence is guaranteed to improve all aspects of your life, especially your relationships with others. It is our ability to identify the emotions and needs of others, along with making an effort to be helpful and provide comfort or support, that predicts the level of intimacy in a relationship.

Visualization Exercise for Creating a Safe Inner Space

The struggles and obstacles that insecure attachment brings with it, like hypervigilance, anxiety, panic attacks, etc., can be exhausting. You may find it hard to switch off sometimes, if ever. Retreating inward to your own safe place can be a great way of reducing stress and helping you feel safe when the world around you feels so chaotic.

Here's how it works:

1. Think about where you want your safe space to be

Construct it in your mind first. I'll share mine with you for this exercise just as an example. You're welcome to use it; just don't move things around. My safe space is in a clearing in a jungle, next to a waterfall that runs into a big, clear pool of water. There's a Bedouin tent with soft rugs, pillows, and bean bags all over where you can sit or lie down to relax. There's always a small table with a serving dish full of fresh fruit. You can hear the howler monkeys and other animals in the distance. There's a type of forcefield that won't allow anything or anyone to enter unless I want them to. So I know I'm completely safe here. It's so peaceful. Sometimes, I take a dip in the pool to cool down, then lie on the cushions to read a book.

2. Practice a script or guided meditation

You have to decide how you'll get to your safe space. You can write down a script and record it to play to yourself or ask someone else to read and record it so you can listen to it like a guided meditation. Or you can download a guided meditation from the many available options online. See a list of resources on the resources page at the end of this book.

3. Practice getting to your safe/calm space

The more you practice getting there, the easier it will be to enter this place of calm and safety that you've created for yourself in your mind. Imagination is a very powerful tool. Have you ever heard of the placebo effect?

4. Make use of it whenever needed

You can choose to enter it whenever you want. Either when you're feeling overwhelmed or on a daily basis as a way of winding down at the end of a day, for example. It is your place to do what you want. No one else needs to know about it, either. It is a place for you to escape to so you can find peace and calm whenever needed.

All these types of exercises have been proven to hold many health benefits, along with teaching yourself how to be more aware, how to be better able to regulate yourself, how to self-soothe, and how to be less responsive to emotional triggers—so you can focus on healing and moving to a place where you are able to build more secure attachments.

An ability that we as adults sadly lose somewhere along the journey of becoming an adult is our ability to play and allow ourselves to be silly. We take ourselves so seriously and forget that our time here is finite. We might as well use it to engage in activities we actually enjoy. In the next chapter, we will look at different types of playful strategies that can help nurture secure attachment.

Chapter 6

Playful Strategies for Secure Attachment

"Being playful naturally liberates the mind, opens the heart, and lifts the spirit. Take time to play today."

Debra L. Reble, Ph.D.

here's a line somewhere along the road to becoming an adult. A line that, once crossed, suddenly makes us think that it's not okay to be playful anymore. It causes us to take life far more seriously than perhaps we should. We forget what it's like to add a little whimsical imagination to our days and be silly enough to laugh at ourselves. Like the late Robin Williams would say, *"You're only given one spark of madness in this life; you mustn't lose it."*

In this chapter, we explore the power of play in therapy and healing. How it can re-awaken parts of ourselves that have laid dormant for so many years, and how creative expression can be the antidote to anxiety.

The Power of Play in Relationships

Play is a crucial part that is lacking in so many relationships today. I'd dare to say it may be one of the contributing factors to today's skyrocketing divorce rates. Play is an important tool that can help with communicating and deepening our connection with one another.

When we think of making time for leisurely activities, it usually results in lying on the couch watching television for hours on end. There's nothing wrong with a bit of television of course, but that time could be spent doing something that is more beneficial to your health, boosts your immune system and creativity, along with strengthening connections.

Play can look like:

- Playing football with your friends.
- Game nights.
- Goofing around with your significant other.
- Playing chess or puzzles.
- Investing in booking activities like river rafting or other fun outdoor experiences.
- Paintball.
- A Nerf war in the house or outside.

There are so many playful activities I can add to the list. It's about finding activities that are fun, enjoyable, and make you laugh more.

Play has many benefits, such as:

- It relieves stress.
- It strengthens your immune system.
- It helps to stimulate the mind and boost creativity.

✧ Being right becomes less important when our focus is on play.

✧ Strengthens bonds.

✧ It can help with communication.

✧ It can help keep intimacy fresh and creative.

✧ Keeps you feeling young and virile.

✧ It stimulates the body and the mind.[42]

Play is also important for boosting all the feel-good neurotransmitters and hormones in your body, like endorphins, dopamine, and oxytocin, that help boost your mood, concentration, memory, and openness.

Playful Communication Exercises

Using play as a communication tool evokes laughter and a sense of having fun, which helps keep relationships exciting and fresh. It's a shared experience of fun that keeps things fresh and helps strengthen your bond and level of intimacy.

Here are some great exercises you can use to strengthen your communication:

Twenty Questions

If you're not familiar with the game, each person gets 20 questions they can ask the other person that they have to answer. All you need is a list of 20 questions, and it can be on any subject. This helps you learn more about the other person (even if you've been together for 50 years, there's always something new to learn), create a sense of fun, and strengthen your bond. Example questions:

✧ What is your favorite of all the dates we've been on together?

✧ When do you feel most appreciated by me?

- ✧ What is your latest pet peeve?

- ✧ What do you wish you had more of in life?

- ✧ Where do you see yourself in 5 years?

- ✧ Etc.

This or That

This game involves you choosing between two options. For example, would you rather have pizza or pasta, winter or summer, indoors or outdoors. This is a great game for couples who haven't been in a relationship for ages, but anyone can play the game.

Don't forget to ask your partner why they chose the answer they did.

Uninterrupted Listening

This is a great game for building better listening skills as well as practicing being more inquisitive. Simply set a timer for 5 minutes. In those five minutes, one of you gets to talk about whatever you want. It can be about your day, it can be a rant, your latest favorite thing, etc. While one partner is talking, the other is not allowed to interrupt. When the timer goes off, you set it again, and the other partner gets to talk about whatever they want to. Remember, while the one is talking, the other is not allowed to interrupt or say anything for that matter. And it's important that you actively listen to what the other person is saying. Pretending to listen while you're thinking about what you will say next defeats the purpose of the exercise. It's about giving one another 100% of your undivided attention.[43]

Try to work some of these in on a weekly basis to help keep things fresh and continue to sharpen your communication skills. See the resources page for more playful communication games.

Managing The "Ick" Response

If you've ever been in a relationship for longer than 3 months, you'll know what I'm referring to when I talk about the "ick" response. When you meet someone new, and it's all butterflies and moonlight strolls, that person can do no wrong. They can slurp their soup or eat crunchy food loudly with their mouth open and you'll think it's adorable.

But once the honeymoon phase is over, these little things suddenly rub you the wrong way to the point where you want to shove the other person down a hole where you'll never have to see them again.

This is called the "ick" response. It's when we feel viscerally triggered by something that someone else does and which we come to see as a turn-off. Like when your partner slurps their soup , and you suddenly feel like you might explode from irritation at any second. It's not uncommon. A poll in the United Kingdom of 2,000 adults showed that almost half of them had dumped someone because of the ick factor.

What's more is, once you have an ick, you carry it with you into other relationships. Let's say you eventually dumped your boyfriend because of his annoying slurping habit. You hit the dating app and set up a dinner date with someone else. When you get to the restaurant, they order a cappuccino, and they *slurp* it up! Immediately, your brain goes into ick mode, and you know that it's over before it even began.

The ick can strike at any time, whether it be 20 years into a marriage or right at the beginning of a new relationship. We're all constantly changing, and so are our preferences. So, something that didn't bother you yesterday may pop up and become a major issue today. It's pretty normal. But why does it happen?

There are a number of reasons this happens, according to psychology.

✧ **Observing red or yellow flags**: As our nervous systems are constantly on the lookout for any danger, certain behaviors in our partners can pop up as sudden red or yellow flags. Red flags are potentially dangerous behavioral cues like any form of abuse. Yellow flags are non-harmful behavior that may not be in alignment with your own values, like someone who is rude to food servers, for example. One of my biggest icks is when someone treats someone else who they believe to be "below their own station" with rudeness or bullying behavior.

✧ **Growing apart**: All relationships have their own seasons, and there may be seasons where you naturally grow apart. One way for your mind to deal with this is to seek out less-favorable aspects of your partner to make it feel like you wouldn't be missing out on much if the relationship came to an end.

✧ **Insecure attachment**: When we struggle to allow ourselves to get close to someone, for whatever reason, the ick can help us feel like we have a legitimate reason for not wanting to open ourselves up or allow ourselves to show any form of vulnerability.

Can you get over the ick?

It depends. In cases where it's because of a red flag you've observed, I'd caution you instead to stay away. You can still work with yellow flags, depending on the other person's willingness to change. Suppose it's because of a lull in your relationship. In that case, you need to sit down and open up communication about what's happening in your relationship and where each of you sees your relationship going. Do you want to remain in the relationship? If so, brainstorm ideas for getting over this hurdle and moving forward.[44]

Creating Playful Rituals

In order for you to create playful rituals, you first need to get in touch with your inner child again. You need to remember what it is that you enjoy doing, what you feel is fun, what makes you laugh, etc.

Let's start with your play type, or your play personality. Dr. Stuart Brown, founder of the National Institute for Play, has developed eight different play personalities through his work. We're all a mix of some of them, but there's usually one that stands out more:

1. **The collector**: Likes to have or hold interesting collections, objects, or experiences.

2. **The competitor**: They love to compete, and they love to win.

3. **The creator/artist**: Likes to play through creative expression and making things.

4. **The director:** They're born organizers and like planning. They like to plan outings, organize parties, organize game nights, etc.

5. **The explorer**: Can be physical, as in visiting a new place. Mental in terms of researching topics like psychology. Or emotional in terms of exploring new emotions, being flirtatious, or deepening a connection, perhaps.

6. **The joker:** The one who likes to be silly and make everyone laugh.

7. **The kinesthete:** Includes people who like to play through movement, like with sports.

8. **The storyteller:** These are imaginative people with a flair for storytelling. This could be in the way of writing, acting, dancing, etc.[45]

Find the quiz in the resources list to explore your own play personality.

You'll be able to identify parts of you in some or all of the above, but one will stand out more than all the others. Can you identify which it is?

Now, how do you create playful rituals?

- ✦ Know your play type by exploring the list above.

- ✦ Find small moments for play on a regular basis.

- ✦ Make a list of things you enjoyed doing as a child and try and incorporate some of it into your daily life. For example, I have a collection of Rubik's cubes, I color, I doodle regularly, and I have playdough on my desk that I can mindlessly play with when I take breaks between writing stints.

- ✦ Do something without sharing it. Social media drives us to do things for the pure purpose of sharing them these days. Do something that is just for yourself and not your following. Create a piece of art, bake a cake, or visit a place you've always wanted to and bask in the feeling of having it all to yourself.

Ask yourself when was the last time that you laughed so hard you could hardly breathe. When was the last time you had fun with your partner or with anyone else? A time you can look back on, and a smile immediately appears on your face? Play doesn't always happen spontaneously in adulthood as it did in childhood. You have to *make time* for it. You also need to retrain yourself because society has trained you to think it's immature or a waste of time to engage in playful activities. A life without play is sad. So is a relationship without play.

Learn how to be more playful and explore areas of yourself that you may have forgotten about. Use it as a way of building stronger connections and a different form of communicating with the people in your life. *"We don't stop playing because we grow old, we grow old because we stop playing."* - George Bernard Shaw

Chapter 7

Building Secure Relationships

"Safety breeds safety. And safe people make us better people for being around them."

Henry Cloud & John Townsend

W hat does a secure relationship look like for you? When you think of the word "security," what does that mean in the sense of a relationship? When all you've ever known is insecure connection, it can be really difficult to answer these questions. When all your body has ever known is stress and vigilance, security and peace can feel completely foreign to the nervous system.

Relationship skills are all those skills that allow you to build healthy and secure relationships. These are skills that are vital for personal well-being, as we all depend on others one way or another and need to be able to foster various relationships in our lives.

Building Relationship Skills

Here are 4 of the main relationship-building skills that you should focus on building first.

1. Emotional Regulation

I've said it before, but this is one of the most important skills to have in life as it allows you to not be a slave to your emotions. It helps you to maintain your composure at times when you feel triggered, and it teaches you how to practice the pause instead of giving in to impulse and engaging in behavior that may damage your relationship.

2. Honesty

Is always the best policy. Even if you want to avoid conflict or spare someone's feelings and feel that honesty will not help, it is always better to be open and honest. Any discomfort or possible conflict that leads from it will give you the opportunity to practice your self-regulation skills, and it will lead to your partner having more trust in you because they know you'll be honest, even if it means it might lead to a potentially bad outcome.

3. Effective Communication

Communication is, of course, also at the top of the list. Without it, you'll never be able to function in any relationship.

4. Active Listening Skills

This means listening to understand instead of simply waiting for the other person to finish talking so you can jump in with your response, having not heard a single word they said.

5. Setting Healthy Boundaries

This is something that most struggle with, but we'll cover boundary-setting skills later on in this chapter.

Let's look at how you can develop each of these skills.

Emotional Regulation Skills

This skill refers to your ability to regulate your inner self when you are feeling intense emotions or when those intense emotions are causing you to feel overwhelmed, like intense anger, intense jealousy, anxiety, panic, etc. Our bodies are designed to react whenever we feel overwhelmed, as it could be a sign of potential danger. To regulate yourself, you need to learn to practice the pause.

Try the following:

- ✧ **Walk away**: It seems pretty obvious but simply removing yourself from the situation can already help with calming down while you practice some deep breathing.

- ✧ **Tip the temperature**: Take a cold shower, hold an ice cube, or run cold water over your face. These help to take your mind off the overwhelming feelings you're experiencing, and the cold temperature helps lower your heart rate, which helps you calm down further.

- ✧ **Practice deep breathing:** Like the breathing techniques I shared with you previously. Breathing is life, and if you're breathing too fast, it causes panic within your body. Practice taking slow, controlled breaths for a few minutes to help regulate your nervous system.

- ✧ **Continue mindfully**: Once you've managed to calm down your nervous system, consider what the best way forward is, then proceed with a calm and contained demeanor.

Honesty

You may immediately think that people who tend to be dishonest are shady people who mean to take advantage of others. This isn't always the case. Sometimes, people with high levels of anxiety lie because they fear confrontation or feel awkward, and lying is the easiest way out of a situation.

- ✧ **Allow yourself to be vulnerable**: As hard as this step can be, you can't be completely honest without allowing at least a bit of vulnerability on your part.

- ✧ **Just do it**: Being open and honest when you think it's going to cause someone to react in a negative way can be hard. Treat it like a Band-Aid. Just rip it off real quick. The longer you take, the more you prolong the agony of wondering what it's going to be like.

- ✧ **Take responsibility**: Admit when you've made a mistake. Making a habit of owning up to your mistakes, and taking whatever consequences they may cause is a great way of garnering greater trust.

- ✧ **Do unto others**: You wouldn't want your friends, family, or significant other lying to you, would you? Treat others as you want to be treated.

We'll be covering the other three points in the sections to come.

Overcoming People-Pleasing and Codependency

This one is especially for those of you who suffer from an anxious or disorganized attachment style. Anyone who has been through experiences in their life that have caused them to believe negative things about themselves, leading to low self-esteem, are people who tend to struggle with people-pleasing and codependency issues in relationships.

Trauma and abuse experienced in childhood can also lead to someone being overly dependent in their relationships, along with struggling to say no when they need to. People-pleasing usually stems from a fear of how someone will react when you say no. In relationships, it can lead to codependency because you do not know how to advocate for yourself and rely on the other person to make all the decisions while you just go along with it. You depend on them for validation and emotional support because you do not know how to provide it for yourself.

Here are 5 ways you can overcome people-pleasing and codependency:

1. **Consider your own needs:** What are YOUR needs in the relationship? Physically and emotionally. You can't effectively communicate your needs until you've taken the time to consider what they are. Take some time sitting with your journal and making a list of your needs and why they are important to you.

2. **Any relationship requires give-and-take:** Ever heard of the saying, "It takes two to tango"? Every relationship is based on a give-and-take practice where both parties engage in both actions. I give you what you need, and you accept what I give. Because I was aware and caring enough to give you what you needed, it's now your turn to give me what I need, and I'll accept it, and so on. If you're the only one doing the giving, you're not in a relationship. You're being treated as a minion who's only there to supply for the other party's needs. And you're worth more than that. Remember, you get what you tolerate.

3. **Learn to find the validation you need within yourself:** Become your own biggest cheerleader. Believe in your skills and abilities and the worth that you bring to this world so you don't need anyone else to provide it for you anymore. This is how you start freeing yourself from others' opinions and learn how to become independent. Realize your potential. Start a business. Take some risks. You only get this life once. Live it your way.

Setting Healthy Boundaries

After emotional regulation, this is my second favorite topic, as it allows you to set yourself free from the shackles you've placed around your own ankles. The shackles are the fear you have of other people's opinions and reactions. You can't protect yourself when you're in shackles and have no shield or weapons of any sort.

You need the following weapons:

- **Start with a small shield:** So many people view boundaries as a battlefield where you need armor up to take on the wrath resulting from your saying no to someone. So, first, you need to train your no-saying muscle with a small shield that's made for small nos. Start with small boundaries, like saying no when you're asked if you want to go out and you really don't want to.

- **Show your weapons from the get-go**: It's a lot easier to set boundaries in a new relationship than in an already established relationship. It can upset the status quo, which is needed sometimes, but it's just a lot easier to say no from the start than to something you've been allowing for a long time.

- ✦ **Sharpen your blade:** This takes consistency. Once you've set a boundary, you need to enforce it whenever someone tries to cross over. There is no negotiating on this. Your boundary is a boundary, and it may not be crossed.

- ✦ **No is a weapon on its own**: The word **no** is a complete sentence. You don't have to explain yourself to anyone. No. Full stop.

- ✦ **Take off your armor**: Engage in regular self-care and self-love time. The business of boundary setting is exhausting and emotionally taxing. But it's a battle worth fighting. Take time out for yourself to replenish your resilience on a regular basis by doing something you enjoy, pamper yourself, and indulge a bit.[47]

Just remember, when you say no to someone else, you are saying yes to yourself. Life is too short to live in fear of how others may react when you stand up for yourself. Don't give your power away so easily. You deserve to take up as much space as you want to.

Effective Communication Strategies

When it comes to effective communication strategies, this, too, is a two-way street. You don't only communicate with yourself; you communicate with the entire world in ways you may not even realize.

Did you know that a great percentage of our communication doesn't even come from words? There are different types of communication, such as:

- ✦ Verbal.

- ✦ Nonverbal.

- ✦ Written.

- ✦ Visual.

- ✦ Listening.

As you'll remember from early on in this book, we established that nonverbal communication often carries far more meaning and impact than any other form of communication. In fact, Albert Mehrabian, Professor Emeritus of Psychology at the University of California, came up with a formula that shows that:

✧ **55%** of our communication is **nonverbal.**

✧ **38%** of our communication is **vocal.** (Tone of voice)

✧ And only **7%** is in the **words** we use.[48]

How we say something is far more important than the actual words that we use. So, the next question then is, knowing all of this, how do you cultivate more effective communication skills?

Here are some helpful tips:

1. Talk slower

We tend to talk faster if we're feeling anxious. Others can feel this because, remember, so much of our communication is nonverbal. Slow down the pace. This will also help you feel calmer. Keep in mind what exactly you're trying to communicate instead of going off on a tangent because you're nervously rambling to get through a potentially uncomfortable situation.

2. Use active, reflective listening

This means that when someone is talking to you, you're giving them your undivided attention and listening in a way that is to understand their point of view better. Don't interrupt them. Give them space to express themselves.

3. Be self-aware

You know your own unhelpful communication patterns. Remind yourself of these so you can overcome them with practice and replace them with more effective communication techniques. For example, shutting down when you feel emotionally overwhelmed. Instead, communicate what you are feeling and that you need a moment to regulate yourself.

4. Focus on the topic at hand

It's tempting to dig up the past and play the blame game when a conversation begins to get heated or seems not to be going the way you had hoped. Stick to the topic at hand. One topic per conversation. If you want to talk about something else, that's for another time. Right now, the conversation is about the one topic at hand.

5. Use "I feel" language

This way, you make it about yourself and do not come at someone in a manner that may cause them to feel attacked. Instead of saying, *"You forgot my birthday. You're so insensitive and forgetful. You don't love me enough even to remember my birthday!"* You could rephrase it as:

- ✧ I feel **hurt.**
- ✧ When you **forget special occasions like my birthday.**
- ✧ Because **it makes me feel like I'm not important enough in your life.**
- ✧ Next time, please **set a reminder on your phone.**

This is a simple script you can use to communicate touchy subjects and personal boundaries more easily. It is a technique used in Dialectical Behavior Therapy to teach effective communication skills.[49]

Healthy over Toxic Relationships

It's great to have all the information on attachment, communication, emotional regulation, mindfulness, and grounding skills– but how does that help you if you aren't able to differentiate between a healthy and a toxic relationship?

Some may think it's obvious, but if all you've ever known is insecurity and dysfunction, how will you know what a healthy relationship looks like?

But first, a word on toxic relationships. Just because someone isn't hitting you, cheating on you, or speaking abusively to you doesn't mean it's not a toxic relationship. You may have a "best friend," for example, who only ever unloads their emotional baggage onto you. You are their emotional punching bag. They never ask how you are or what they can do to help you. They constantly ask for advice but never implement any of the advice you give them. They're stuck in a victim mentality, and you're the sucker they're offloading on because you allow it. This, too, is an example of a toxic relationship. Any kind of one-sided relationship is bound to be a toxic one.

Here are 5 main differences between a toxic and a healthy relationship:

1. Conflict Resolution

Couples who are able to openly discuss and talk through any conflict to find a mutually acceptable solution are signs of a mature and healthy relationship. In a toxic relationship, the only type of conflict resolution tools that get used are screaming, manipulating, passive-aggressive behavior, or silent treatment.

2. How You Talk About Your Partner

Gossiping about your partner or talking negatively about them behind their back or vice versa is a clear sign of a toxic relationship. A healthy relationship is one where both partners respect one another, and your partner is also your friend. You lift each other up and always have one another's back. (Unless they're doing something wrong or immoral, then you should be able to hold them accountable)

3. Apologies

Mature and emotionally intelligent individuals are able to own up to their own mistakes and apologize for their wrongdoings. What's even more important than an apology is changed behavior. An apology means nothing without it. In toxic relationships, apologies either happen rarely or are only given by a victim in a toxic relationship to prevent an abuser from hurting them. Or both parties just refuse to apologize and take responsibility for their actions, which means the relationship will never be able to move forward.

4. Relationship Equality

In a healthy relationship, both partners are equals. Both of your needs are important, valued, and provided for. Your opinions are equally important. You compromise to meet each other's needs and share your lives with one another. In a toxic relationship, one person is always more important than the other. One person sees themselves as the dominant figure in the relationship and expects the other to be their servant. You see this especially in narcissistic abusive relationships.

5. You Share a Safe Space

Your home and your relationship should be a place of comfort and trust. You should be able to be yourself and openly express your thoughts, emotions, and needs. In a healthy relationship, you're able to do this. Your relationship is your safe haven. A place where you know you have an equal partner who's in it for the long run with you. In a toxic relationship, it's a jungle out there and in here. What you share is sometimes held against you or used to hurt you somewhere down the road. You're not able to safely express your true self and need to wear a mask everywhere you go for your own safety.[50]

Conflict Resolution Techniques

The ability to resolve conflict is crucial in any relationship. Whether it's at work, at home, among friends or family, it doesn't matter. No relationship can be balanced and healthy when no conflict resolution occurs.

Issues are sometimes left for too long or ignored completely, leading to resentment on one or both parties' fronts. A sign of emotional intelligence, maturity, and respect is when someone can sit down to discuss an issue calmly and respectfully while trying to find a solution that will work for both parties involved.

Here are some helpful strategies and techniques you can implement for better communication and conflict resolution in your relationship.

1.   Agree to a win-win solution

It's important to remember that you're on the same team. You're not enemies fighting on opposite sides of a war. This is your relationship, and the best way to resolve conflict is to go in with a win-win mindset. Before you start discussing the issue at hand, agree that you are both on the same page, which is to find a solution that works for both of you.

2.   Regular Check-Ins

Agree to do regular couple check-ins to gauge where your relationship is and whether there's anything you need to talk about or resolve. It's easier to keep communication channels open and take care of any small conflicts as you go instead of waiting for more issues to build up inside of you until you erupt like Mount Vesuvius.

3.   Remove Disturbances in the Relationship

This means making a list of existing relationship disagreements and conflicts along with the emotional reactions that accompany them. It might be more helpful to describe these as triggers. Topics, issues, and behaviors that can derail a conversation when you're in the middle of resolving a conflict. For example, when they interrupt you mid-sentence and talk over you without giving you a chance to finish your sentence. This is the kind of thing that can make someone shut down emotionally and not be open for discussion anymore.

4. Time Out

Agree that you are both allowed to call a time-out if emotions are getting to a level where they are overwhelming. You cannot communicate effectively in this state. It's better to take 5 or 10 minutes apart to cool down, then come back together to continue together mindfully.[51]

Fostering Trust in Relationships

There are few things as comforting in this world as knowing that you have someone in your life who you can trust with your emotions and vulnerability. Someone who you can count on to not break the trust you have. It is only in the presence of trust that we can truly allow ourselves to be open and vulnerable with another, knowing that they will not use it against us or try to use it to hurt us in some way, as so often happens in insecure relationships.

I would go as far as to say that there is nothing more important than trust in a relationship. Trust helps promote closeness, helps with conflict resolution skills that we just covered, and it promotes a sense of positivity within the relationship.

When trust is lacking in a relationship, it often leads to:

✧ Feeling insecure within the relationship.

✧ Fixating on the negative or feeling resentful towards your partner.

✧ A fear of abandonment or fear for your safety, depending on the circumstance.

✧ Feeling lonely within the relationship.

✧ A sense of distress, knowing you can't trust the person closest to you.

So, how can you work on deepening the trust in your relationship?

1. Open Communication

Engaging in open communication is the only way of letting your partner know how you feel. When there is a sense of secrecy between you, there will always be a lack of trust. Talk about what is bothering you openly and agree to work together to be more open with one another.

2. Consistency is Key

You both need to keep and follow through on any commitments you make to one another. Consistency builds trust and can rebuild trust even in relationships where there has never been any. It takes time to win someone's trust, so be patient and remain consistent.

3. Find Ways to Connect

When you make a concerted effort to connect with one another on a regular basis, there is a sense of value in the relationship. You value one another enough to put time and effort into connecting with one another. This strengthens your bond and can help you better communicate and build greater levels of trust.

4. Listen Empathically

Remember when we covered the section on active listening and listening to understand and not just respond? Listening in an empathetic manner means listening to someone in an inquisitive way that makes you want to understand where they are coming from. You want to try and see things from their point of view. Try and put yourself in your partner's shoes when they communicate with you. Feeling heard helps you place more trust in someone as you feel they value you enough as a person to take true note of what you're saying.

5. Create New Positive Experiences

Sometimes, you need to change the pace to freshen up or liven up your relationship again. It's only natural for relationships to go through their own form of ebbing and flowing. When it's a relationship where there has never been much trust, creating new positive experiences together can help bring you closer together, strengthen your bond, deepen your intimacy, and help you build trust anew.[52]

Trust is an incredibly important part of any relationship, especially for people who have experienced adversity, abuse, or trauma in childhood. Those who have developed insecure attachment styles in adulthood will always need extra reassurance and an extra helping of patience from their partner to gain their trust.

Evolving as a Person

They say people never change. It's not true on any level. We are all constantly changing– physically, emotionally, and psychologically. Our bodies change as we get older, meaning they might need a different type of nutrition and exercise. We (not all) become more mature, and our priorities change all the time as we make our way through this rollercoaster of a ride that we call life.

Emotionally, people either evolve, devolve, or stagnate. And unless you have a neurological condition that prevents you from being able to make your own decisions, it's always a choice.

I saw an internet trend some time ago that said: "Choose your hard."

"Relationships are hard, divorce is hard; choose your hard."

"Exercising is hard, weakened bones and muscles are hard; choose your hard."

"Eating healthy is hard, being sick is hard; choose your hard."

You get the idea.

What's important is that you realize that you are always just one step away from becoming a completely new person. At any given moment in your life, you can choose to change any aspect of yourself.

Changing your habits in a relationship is hard, being in a toxic relationship is hard; choose your hard. Get help. Do whatever it is you need to do to ensure your (and your children's, if you have any) freedom.

Choose to invest in yourself every single day. Do the work. Learn from your mistakes. Live with a purposeful sense of curiosity. Set goals for yourself. Write down your top 5 goals. Then erase the four numbers below number 1, and just focus on that one until you achieve it. Then, move on to the next item on your list.

Go for therapy. The right therapist will be able to guide you along your healing journey with compassion and understanding. I believe that everyone can benefit from therapy at least once a month. If the world was in therapy, we'd be in a better place.

Learn to be kinder to yourself. In the end, you're all you've got. Learn to be comfortable by yourself. It's an incredibly empowering skill to have. When you are comfortable on your own, you are unstoppable. I'm not saying you should be alone. I'm saying you should be able to be alone unless someone magnificent and worthy of your time comes along. That's right. Start thinking in terms of whether other people are worth your time and effort. Do they deserve your attention, your hope, your trust?

Invest in yourself and your personal growth on an ongoing basis. You only get to live this life once, no matter what you believe. Live with intention and stop allowing the opinions of others to pull you down.

You are worthy of love, kindness, understanding, and protection.

Chapter 8

Unleashing Emotional Intelligence

*"Emotional Intelligence grows through perception.
Look around at your present situation and observe it
through the level of feeling."*

Deepak Chopra.

We touched on the topic of emotional intelligence previously. In this chapter, we take a more in-depth look at how it impacts our lives, how you can identify areas related to your own emotional intelligence that you need to work on, and tools and strategies to assist you in doing just that.

As always, it all starts with awareness.

Emotional Awareness and Regulation

As your self-awareness grows, so will your emotional awareness. As you put the tools I've shared with you in this book to use on a regular basis, you'll become more aware of your own emotional triggers and responses. This will eventually translate into having the ability to catch yourself before automatically responding to an emotion you are feeling in a way that might cause a negative impact on your life, even if it's in a small way.

In order to be able to regulate our emotions effectively, we first need to be able to correctly identify what it is we're feeling. There is a wide spectrum of emotions, and often, the emotion you think you're struggling with might not be the primary emotion at all.

There are primary and secondary emotions. Secondary emotions stem from a primary emotion. For example, see if you can identify which is the primary and which is the secondary emotion in the following story. Joanne is the CEO of a large corporation. She's known as a stern but fair leader with a strong sense of compassion for the people who work with and for her. She's been feeling a little under the weather, and today, when Ronald came into her office to admit to a mistake he had made on the annual report, Joanne lost her cool and went off at him for the entire office to hear. Later, she felt really bad about losing her temper like that and apologized to both Ronald and everyone who had to bear witness to her outburst.

So? Can you tell which is which?

- ✧ Primary emotion = **Anger**
- ✧ Secondary emotion = **Shame**

Look at this wheel of emotions. It shows the common primary emotions we feel, and the secondary and even tertiary feelings that can stem from our primary emotions.

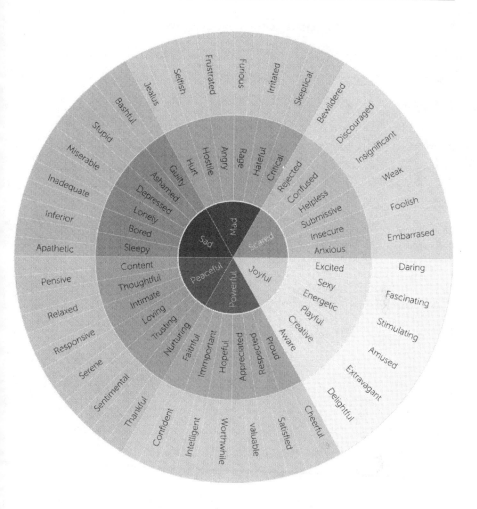

Improving your emotional vocabulary will help you better identify what it is you're actually feeling. Then, you can take a step back to practice self-regulation or self-soothing techniques to help you process that emotion before you move forward with a behavioral response.

Studies have shown that people who have a lower level of emotional awareness tend to suffer from higher rates of anxiety and depression compared to people with a greater sense of emotional awareness.[54]

How do you foster emotional awareness?

Keep a mood diary for the next 30 days. Get yourself a journal and carry it with you wherever you go. You can also use digital means like your phone or a tablet. Throughout the day, whenever you notice yourself experiencing an emotion, make a note of it, along with the day of time and what was going on around you when you felt this emotion. So, you need 3 columns:

Emotion	Time of day	Circumstance
Anxiety	11:45	Getting ready for a meeting.
Happy	17:00	Packing up to go home.

I know there are only two times in this table, which makes it look like this person only had two emotions for the entire day. It's just an example, obviously.

Keeping a mood diary can give you insight into the types of emotions you tend to experience most, as well as clue you in on the cause for some of them. The example above doesn't give us enough data to enable us to make certain assumptions. But for example's sake, the anxiety experienced while getting ready to go into a meeting might mean that meetings cause you to feel anxious, or maybe someone in that meeting causes you anxiety, or perhaps you just get anxious in group settings in general.

Your homework: Keep a mood diary for at least the next 30 days. After the 30 days are over, look back over your notes and see if you can identify any patterns or explanations for certain emotions that you experience. Also, try to identify primary vs secondary emotions.

Refer back to Chapter 3 where we covered different emotional regulation skills you can implement to help you self-soothe when you are experiencing intense emotions.

Empathetic Listening and Empathy Building

Empathy allows us to understand others on a deeper level, especially the different people we are in relationships with. It also gifts us the ability to build stronger connections with others. It's basically the ability to imagine what it would be like if you were in someone else's shoes. What might it feel like if you were going through what someone else is going through? For example, someone just lost their job and has four children at home to look after. What do you imagine that person might be feeling right now? Well, it's impossible to really know what they're feeling, but we can imagine that they may feel distraught, afraid, disappointed, and panicked. That's how most people would probably feel.

Having this ability to consider what someone else might be thinking or feeling in the situations they find themselves in will allow you to build greater empathy for others, which is the first step to learning how to practice empathetic listening.

How to practice empathetic listening:

Empathetic listening is similar to active listening. It's the art of listening more than you speak, but not just listening for the sake of listening. You're listening to try and better understand what the other person is feeling, what they're experiencing, and what they're currently going through. So often, we have no idea what others are going through behind closed doors. We all put on our social masks when we go out to make it seem like everything is all good and dandy out of fear of judgment or pity. It's important to understand that empathy has nothing to do with pity. Pity is feeling sorry *for*, whereas empathy is feeling sorry *with*.

When you're practicing empathetic listening, try not to interrupt the person who is speaking. Simply nod or use confirming phrases like "I see" or "I understand." When they are done talking, and you have the opportunity to reflect on what they've said, ask them probing questions like, "Am I understanding you correctly when I say you felt ..." or questions like "Why did it make you feel that way..." or "Why is that important to you..." etc. This helps give you more insight into why they are feeling the way they are feeling or why they struggle with the things they struggle with.

Asking probing questions will also help encourage them to keep talking so you can continue practicing your empathetic listening skills. You want the other person to feel heard without being judged. This is how you know you've successfully listened in an empathetic manner.[55]

Allowing others to feel heard is essential for bonding and connection in relationships, so this is an important skill to practice. Empathy for others is important, but what about empathy for self?

Developing Empathy for Self

We tend to be our own worst critics and can be harder on ourselves than anyone else would ever be. A crucial part of learning how to be a more empathetic person for the purposes of building deeper connections and trust in your relationships is learning how to develop empathy for self.

Answer this question: Do you treat yourself the same way you treat your favorite person in your life? If the answer is no, you need to practice more empathy for yourself.

How often do you judge or criticize yourself in your mind, saying things like: "You suck," "You're so ugly," "You'll never amount to anything," or "You're so stupid" ? What message do you think you are sending to yourself, your mind, and your body when you think and say these things? It's not a good one. And it certainly isn't true.

Remember, thoughts are just thoughts, not facts, and you can change the way you think. It all starts with you.

Here are some tips to help you improve your empathy-for-self skills

1. Stop Comparing

Don't compare yourself to others. You are uniquely you and the aim of life isn't to be like anyone else. It's to learn how to be 100% authentically yourself and be comfortable with who you are.

2. Forgive Yourself

We all make mistakes. Forgive yourself for mistakes you've made in the past and in the present. This doesn't mean that you're excusing your behavior. Own up to and accept responsibility for any mistakes that you make, but start viewing them as the learning opportunities that they are. Mistakes are good, as long as you learn from them and change for the better.

3. Stop Self-Judgment

Use tools like mindfulness and meditation to practice letting go of self-judgment. Face the parts of yourself that you do not like and either accept them or do something about them. If you're not doing something about it, it means that you accept it. You are fallible, just like every other human being on this planet. The good news is that there's always room for growth.

4. Talk to Yourself Like You Would Your Best Friend

Would you tell your best friend that they are stupid or useless? Some people do it in a joking manner. But would you tell your friends that they are stupid or useless and really mean it? It wouldn't make you much of a friend if you said yes, would it? Be as understanding with yourself as you are with the people you love the most. Learn to talk to yourself kindly. Like you would like others to talk to you.[56]

The world is a harsh enough place as it is without you having to add more pressure on yourself. Learn to be kinder to yourself and practice greater self-empathy on a daily basis. Remember what I said before: you cannot give what you do not have. Build up your reserves, then give to others what you do not need because you have enough for yourself.

Journaling for Self-Regulation

Journaling is one of my favorite tools for all things personal development. Want to understand yourself better? Journal. Want to understand someone else better? Journal. Want to get rid of unwanted, hurtful thoughts and emotions? Journal. Want to become more self-aware? Journal. Want to come up with ideas? Journal. You get the idea. I love journaling as a tool for almost any and all issues we struggle with in life. Except if it's something that requires physical, professional intervention.

Journaling is this space where you can explore all aspects of yourself and life. We, so often, need to keep our composure and live under the masks I referred to earlier, but in your journal, you can express yourself truly and freely.

It's a fantastic tool that can help you explore thoughts and emotions you are struggling with and provides you with an opportunity to reconnect with yourself.

People often struggle to get started. The main struggles I usually hear are:

✧ I don't know what to say.

✧ I don't know how to write.

✧ I don't know where to start.

You can use your journal for whatever reason you want. You can use it as an info-dumping tool at the end of each day to clear out your mind. You can use it as a tool to explore particular emotions you are struggling with and figure out where they stem from. You can use it to just write about your day on a daily basis or to keep track of your thought patterns. It is such a simple yet versatile tool. Above all, it can help by providing you with a "space" to express yourself by writing down what you are thinking and feeling so you can get rid of any pent-up emotions, thus aiding in self-regulation. Your journal is like a checkpoint between yourself and the rest of the world. It can help you make sense of things by acting as a soundboard of sorts.

I know it can be difficult to get started if you've never engaged in the art of journaling before, so here are some prompts to get you going:

- ✧ Which emotions am I trying to avoid?

- ✧ Why am I trying to deny or avoid this emotion?

- ✧ What is keeping me from addressing and processing what I am feeling right now?

- ✧ What purpose does being hard on myself serve?

- ✧ What benefits would I gain from being kinder to myself?

- ✧ What would it sound like if I spoke to myself in the manner I wished my parents did?

- ✧ What have I learned about myself in the relationship I am currently in?

- ✧ What did I learn from the relationship I was in? (If you just got out of a relationship)

- ✧ What have my experiences up until now taught me about what I want in a life partner?

- ✧ What needs do I have that I am not fulfilling for myself?

- ✧ What relationship needs do I have that my partner isn't fulfilling?

- ✧ Why am I in my current relationship?

- ✧ What is causing me to feel what I am feeling, and what can I do about it?

- ✧ What are all the things I love about myself?

- ✧ How can I help myself not be so reactive to certain triggers anymore?[57]

These are some great prompts to get you going and really dig into getting to know yourself better, getting to know your triggers, your needs, your thoughts, your emotions, what you want, and what you don't want. As you become more self-aware, you'll have a greater capacity for regulating yourself whenever you need to.

Practicing Vulnerability and Open Communication

A no-go zone for most people who have lived through some form of abuse or trauma in their lives. For someone who has lived through circumstances that have caused them to adopt an insecure attachment style, vulnerability is like the boogeyman. It's a very scary thing that can hurt you. Yet we need to be able to allow ourselves to be vulnerable in our relationships and to let others in so we can foster deeper connections. A relationship without any vulnerability is not a relationship at all. It's like an empty box. When you start putting things into this box that you share with someone else, that's when you're adding to the relationship. You both put things into the box, trusting that neither of you will take from the box with the intention of hurting the other or using it against them somewhere down the line in the future.

That's usually the main fear that stands in someone's way of allowing themselves to be vulnerable with someone else. Trust is a prerequisite for vulnerability. Without trust, there can be no sharing of self. Well, there can be, but then you're not sharing in a safe space, which usually ends badly–for you.

Vulnerability can help boost your confidence as it increases your belief in yourself and that you can handle difficult situations. It helps build stronger relationships as it deepens intimacy, and it helps you to embrace and accept different aspects of yourself.

How to practice being more vulnerable:

1. Start with Why

First, figure out why this is important to you. Why do you feel the need to be vulnerable about this particular experience with this particular person? Or do you want to be more vulnerable with others so you can strengthen and deepen your connections with the people in your life? Not everyone deserves your vulnerability.

2. Embrace Your Authentic Self

In order for you to make yourself vulnerable in a safe manner, it's best that you first learn to embrace and accept yourself, flaws and all. A fear of vulnerability usually stems from pain inflicted upon us in the past. This treatment may have caused you to form certain beliefs about yourself that have made you judge and criticize yourself up until now. To undo this, you need to practice self-love, compassion, and acceptance in order to embrace your authentic self. Look into a mirror every day and tell yourself 3 things you like about yourself. Practice the butterfly hug that we discussed on a regular basis. Journal about how you see and feel about yourself. All these exercises can help you learn how to embrace and accept yourself for the unique and worthy person you are.

3. Communicate Openly

If someone does something that hurts you or makes you feel unsafe, let them know by speaking up and advocating for yourself. Even if the other person is doing so without realizing what they're doing is making you uncomfortable. It doesn't matter. They cannot read your mind, so you need to use your words and use them in a way that leaves no room for doubt. You can't expect people to read your mind; you need to teach them how you want to be treated.

4. Seek Professional Help

There's a lot of work you can do on your own, but you don't know what you don't know, and we all have blind spots. A skilled, licensed mental health professional will be able to gently guide you along your path of healing in a manner that helps you discover answers for yourself. If you've been to therapy before and it didn't work for you, try again. I see too many people throwing in the towel after one measly 60-minute session. If you don't feel comfortable with your current therapist, change. You're not a tree with roots, you can go wherever you want. The right professional for you can make a massive difference in your life. You'll know when you've found the right one for you. They'll also be able to help you with the following point.[58]

Building Emotional Bridges in Relationships

Emotional communication is essential to any relationship. Trust begins and ends with emotional communication. A relationship is like a ceramic pot. Every time you break someone's trust or vice versa, a piece breaks off, and the relationship is never quite the same again. The more this happens, the more cracks appear, and the more pieces break off. Although the relationship can never take on the same form, there is hope as long as both parties want to rebuild what has been broken down.

The Japanese art of Kintsugi is the art of using gold to put broken pottery back together. The philosophy behind the technique is that one should embrace one's own flaws and imperfections and that, with some effort, you can rebuild something even stronger and more beautiful.[59]

Here are some things you can try to rebuild broken bridges in your various relationships, but especially in your relationship with your significant other.

- ✧ Do more things together.
- ✧ Hug more often.
- ✧ Kiss each other more often.
- ✧ Bring your partner coffee in bed.
- ✧ Sign up for a class together– it could be clay sculpting, cooking, whatever tickles your fancy.
- ✧ Practice those active listening skills. Listen more than you talk.
- ✧ Surprise them with a thoughtful gift.
- ✧ Show them appreciation daily.
- ✧ Take a spontaneous trip somewhere.
- ✧ Talk over a glass of wine or coffee and a game, like chess, checkers, cards, backgammon, etc.

✧ Make a list of fun things you each have always wanted to do, then cut them up into individual pieces and put them in a bowl to fish out of. Every month, pick something from the bowl and go and do it.

✧ Leave them a love note.

✧ Tend to your partner when they're ill.

✧ Remember small details of what they like, like how they like their coffee, their favorite chocolate, etc. Then, buy it for them or make their coffee just the way they like it and serve it with their favorite chocolate, etc.

Find ways to open communication, show each other appreciation and kindness, have fun, be compassionate, show understanding, be attentive, and put those pieces back together slowly, one piece at a time.

Becoming a Happier You

I've said this before multiple times in this book. In the end, your happiness is your own responsibility. It's something that comes from within and not something to go and search for in others. To become a happier, better version of yourself, you need to be brave enough to take a good, long, hard look at yourself to identify the areas you need to work on that have been holding you back first. Rome wasn't built in a day, and personal development is a lifelong journey. The goal is to be just 1% better at something than you were at it yesterday.

Invest in understanding yourself better, whether it's through personal exploration by yourself or working with a professional who can help guide you on your journey. Knowledge is power, but understanding is even more important. By doing the work that will enable you to answer the question "why," you'll empower yourself with so many insights along the way. Questions like, "Why do I struggle with this?" "Why am I like this?" "Why do I keep repeating this cycle?" "Why does this trigger me?" etc. Curiosity, consistency, and compassion are key. Let's call it the three C's.

See yourself as an adventurer on a journey to discover the treasure that is your authentic self. The version of you who isn't afraid to say no. The version of you who can communicate what you want with confidence. The version of you who looks after your health in every aspect. The version of you who doesn't stay in a relationship where they aren't treated with respect and understanding. The version of you who is not afraid to take up space anymore.

You are not a mistake. Do you know the odds of you existing? They're stupendous. You were meant to be here. For some reason, you have had to walk the path that you've been on until you discovered this book. Now, you know that you have a choice. You don't have to stay on this path. You can change direction any moment you want to.

The healing journey is one filled with many twists and turns. It is hard, and it is messy. Which is why so few people dare embark on the journey. They're afraid, with reason. But that being said, it is the most empowering and fulfilling work there is in this life. Mending the parts of yourself that have been covered with band-aids for years or buried deep down in the muck of a traumatic past.

Become the person you would've felt safe with when you were a child. You owe yourself that. Because you are worth it.

CONCLUSION

This book is only the beginning. Perhaps you've read other similar books. I firmly believe that every person, every circumstance, and every tool that crosses our path carries something new for us to learn.

The next step is to keep practicing what you have learned here in this book. Engage in all the exercises and put all these new tools you've been equipped with in your toolbox of life for when you need them going forward.

You now know what attachment styles are and where they stem from, and you have had the opportunity to identify your own if you haven't done so previously. You should have better insight into how different attachment styles impact your life in different ways, especially in your relationships.

We've covered anxious attachment in-depth, and you now know that there are certain aspects of your biology that also drive your behavior. Beyond this, you now know how to identify your emotions and how to regulate those emotions more effectively. You now know what to do when you are feeling overwhelmed, but remember, it takes regular practice to be able to instantly access one of your self-soothing tools without needing to think about it too much.

We've talked about how automatic negative thoughts can infiltrate your life in a big way, how intense emotions can wreak havoc in your relationships, and how giving in to a knee-jerk reaction can cause lasting damage. But, more importantly, you now have the answers in hand that will teach you how to change all of this.

Practicing mindfulness, meditation, and grounding techniques on a regular basis will help keep you balanced and regulated while you do the inner work needed to overcome insecure attachment, which will allow you to foster deeper connections and greater trust in your relationships.

You have everything you need to live your best life within yourself. It's okay if you struggle some days. It's part of the journey. If you feel like you need help, reach out and ask for it, whether it be from a friend, family member, or a licensed professional who is trained to help when you feel stuck.

My wish for you is that you will keep engaging in this work courageously so you can heal yourself and live the life you have always dreamed of.

Go out and live the kind of life that "little you" would be proud of.

I truly hope you enjoyed this book and that you have found some value in the information I have shared here with you. I would really appreciate it if you'd consider leaving an honest review so I can share my work with as many people who are in need of this information.

Thank you.

HELPFUL RESOURCES

Cognitive Distortions

https://positivepsychology.com/cognitive-distortions/

Complex-PTSD

https://psychcentral.com/ptsd/complex-ptsd

https://www.verywellmind.com/what-is-complex-ptsd-2797491

https://www.healthline.com/health/cptsd

Breathing Exercises

https://www.healthline.com/health/breathing-exercise

https://positivepsychology.com/breathing-exercises/

Meditation Resources

https://positivepsychology.com/meditation-exercises-activities/

https://www.health.harvard.edu/alternative-and-integrative-health/two-mindfulness-meditation-exercises-to-try

More Communication Games

https://www.marriage.com/advice/communication/easy-games-that-can-help-fix-bad-communication/

Your Play Personality

https://www.nifplay.org/what-is-play/play-personalities/

REFERENCES

[1] National Collaborating Centre for Mental Health (UK). (2015, November). Children's attachment: Attachment in children and young people who are adopted from care, in care or at high risk of going into care. National Institute for Health and Care Excellence (NICE). (NICE Guideline, No. 26). https://www.ncbi.nlm.nih.gov/books/NBK356196/

McLeod, S., Ph.D. (2023, November 30). *John Bowlby's Attachment Theory*. Simply Psychology. Retrieved January 2, 2024, from https://www.simplypsychology.org/bowlby.html

[2] Harlow, H. F., Dodsworth, R. O., & Harlow, M. K. (1965). Total social isolation in monkeys. *Proceedings of the National Academy of Sciences of The United States of America*, 54(1), 90–97. https://doi.org/10.1073/pnas.54.1.90

[3] Rosmalen, Lenny & van der Veer, René & van der Horst, Frank. (2015). Ainsworth's Strange Situation Procedure: The origin of an instrument. Journal of the History of the Behavioral Sciences. 51. DOI:10.1002/jhbs.21729

[4] Sim, S., Shin, J. E., & Sohn, Y. W. (2019). Effects of Non-verbal Priming on Attachment-Style Activation. *Psychology for Clinical Settings*, 10. https://doi.org/10.3389/fpsyg.2019.00684

Huang, S. (2023, November 23). *Attachment Styles And How They Affect Adult Relationships*. Simply Psychology. Retrieved January 13, 2024, from https://www.simplypsychology.org/attachment-styles.html#Attachment-In-Adult-Relationships

The Attachment Project (2023, July 29). *Attachment Styles & Their Role in Relationships*. Retrieved January 13, 2024, from https://www.attachmentproject. com/blog/four-attachment-styles/

[5] Resnick, A., CSC. (2023, April 13). *Signs of Dismissive Avoidant Attachment*. Verywell Mind. Retrieved February 1, 2024, from https://www.verywellmind.com/what-is-dismissive-avoidant-attachment-5218213

[6] Bond, S., & Bond, M. (2005). Attachment Styles and Violence Within Couples. The Journal of Nervous and Mental Disease, 192, 857-863. https://doi.org/10.1097/01. nmd.0000146879.33957.ec

[7] Greene, R. (2023, June 20). What Disorganized Attachment Looks Like in a Relationship. Verywell Mind. Retrieved February 1, 2024, from https://www.verywellmind.com/ disorganized-attachment-in-relationships-7500701

[8] Mandriota, M. (2021, October 13). *Here Is How to Identify Your Attachment Style*. Psych Central. Retrieved January 13, 2024, from https://psychcentral.com/health/4-attachment-styles-in-relationships#disorganized-attachment

Ha, L. (2021, November 11). *Recognizing Our Attachment Style Can Help Us in Our Relationships*. Stanford Couples Counseling. Retrieved January 13, 2024, from https://www.stanfordcouplescounseling.com/recognizing-our-attachment-style-can-help-us-in-our-relationships/

Levy, T. (2020, June 22). *What is your attachment style? Understanding adult attachment patterns*. Evergreen Psychotherapy Center. Retrieved January 13, 2024, from https://evergreenpsychotherapycenter.com/what-is-your-attachment-style-understanding-adult-attachment-patterns/

[9] Lebow, H. I. (2022, June 22). *How an anxious attachment style affects relationships*. Psych Central. Retrieved January 15, 2024, from https://psychcentral.com/health/ anxious-attachment-style-signs#impact-on-relationships

Cafasso, J. (2019, November 14). *What Is Anxious Attachment?* Healthline. Retrieved February 1, 2024, from https://www.healthline.com/health/mental-health/ anxious-attachment

[10] Marshall, A., PsyD (2023, May 3). *Signs You Have an Anxious-Preoccupied Attachment Style*. Verywell Mind. Retrieved February 2, 2024, from https://www.verywellmind. com/what-is-preoccupied-attachment-style-5214833

[11] (n.d.). *Relationship 101: Questions To Ask To Learn About Your Upbringing & Attachment Style*. Liberation Healing Seattle. Retrieved February 2, 2024, from https://www. liberationhealingseattle.com/blog-trauma-therapist/questions-to-ask-to-learn-about-your-upbringing-attachment-style

[12] Herndon, J., MS., MPH., MFA. (2021, August 9). *Having Anxiety vs. Feeling Anxious: What's the Difference?* Healthline. Retrieved February 2, 2024, from https://www. healthline.com/health/anxiety/anxiety-vs-anxious

[13] Silva Casabianca, S. (2022, January 11). *15 Cognitive Distortions To Blame for Negative Thinking*. Psych Central. Retrieved February 2, 2024, from https://psychcentral. com/lib/cognitive-distortions-negative-thinking

[14] Saxena, S., MBA., MSW., LSW., CCTP. (2022, October 18). *Anxious Attachment: Definition, Causes, & Signs*. Choosing Therapy. Retrieved February 2, 2024, from https://www.choosingtherapy.com/anxious-attachment/

[15] Gottschalk, M. G., & Domschke, K. (2017). Genetics of generalized anxiety disorder and related traits. Dialogues in clinical neuroscience, 19(2), 159–168. https://doi. org/10.31887/DCNS.2017.19.2/kdomschke

[16] Ross A. Thompson, Jeffry A. Simpson & Lisa J. Berlin (2022) Taking perspective on attachment theory and research: nine fundamental questions, Attachment & Human Development, 24:5, 543-560, DOI: 10.1080/14616734.2022.2030132

[17] Holmes, J., & Slade, A. (2019). The neuroscience of attachment: implications for psychological therapies. The British Journal of Psychiatry, 214(6), 318–319. doi:10.1192/bjp.2019.7

(n.d.). *Neuroscience of Human Attachment*. Frontiers. Retrieved February 2, 2024, from https://www.frontiersin.org/research-topics/3053/neuroscience-of-human-attachment/articles

[18] Ryder, G. (2022, January 19). *What Is Attachment Trauma?* Psych Central. Retrieved February 2, 2024, from https://psychcentral.com/health/attachment-trauma#causes

Lahousen, T., Unterrainer, H. F., & Kapfhammer, H. P. (2019). Psychobiology of Attachment and Trauma-Some General Remarks From a Clinical Perspective. Frontiers in psychiatry, 10, 914. https://doi.org/10.3389/fpsyt.2019.00914

[19] Kenneth Lee Raby, Mary Dozier, Attachment across the lifespan: insights from adoptive families, Current Opinion in Psychology, Volume 25, 2019, Pages 81-85, ISSN 2352-250X, https://doi.org/10.1016/j.copsyc.2018.03.011.

McConnell, M. & Moss, E.. (2011). Attachment across the life span: Factors that contribute to stability and change. Australian Journal of Educational and Developmental Psychology. 11. 60-77.

[20] Comninos, A., Ph.D. (n.d.). *How Your Attachment Style Affects Your Emotion Regulation & Relationships.* Mindfulness and Clinical Psychology Solutions. Retrieved February 2, 2024, from https://mi-psych.com.au/how-attachment-affects-your-emotion-regulation-relationships/

Cassidy J. (1994). Emotion regulation: influences of attachment relationships. *Monographs of the Society for Research in Child Development, 59*(2-3), 228–249.

[21] Borchard, T. J. (2011, June 28). *Marsha Linehan: What is Dialectical Behavioral Therapy (DBT)?* Psych Central. Retrieved February 2, 2024, from https://psychcentral.com/blog/marsha-linehan-what-is-dialectical-behavioral-therapy-dbt#1

[22] Mooventhan, A., Bharti, S., Nivethitha, L., & Manjunath, N. K. (2021). Effect of Ice Massage to Head and Spine on Blood Pressure and Heart Rate Variability in Patients with Hypertension: a Pilot Study. International journal of therapeutic massage & bodywork, 14(3), 22–26. https://doi.org/10.3822/ijtmb.v14i3.573

[23] Lebow, H. I., & Silva Casabianca, S. (2022, April 6). *Do You Know How to Manage Your Emotions and Why It Matters?* Psych Central. Retrieved February 2, 2024, from https://psychcentral.com/health/emotional-regulation#skills

(n.d.). *Emotion Regulation.* DBT Self Help. Retrieved February 2, 2024, from https://dbtselfhelp.com/dbt-skills-list/emotion-regulation/

[24] Feuerman, M., LCSW., LMFT., (2022, December 5). *Coping With an Insecure Attachment Style*. Verywell Mind. Retrieved February 14, 2024, from https://www.verywellmind.com/marriage-insecure-attachment-style-2303303

[25] Pelly, J. (2019, September 27). *What Is Avoidant Attachment?* Healthline. Retrieved February 14, 2024, from https://www.healthline.com/health/parenting/avoidant-attachment#what-causes-it

[26] (2023, June 5). *Disorganized Attachment: Causes & Symptoms*. Attachment Project. Retrieved February 14, 2024, from https://www.attachmentproject.com/blog/disorganized-attachment/

[27] Cleveland Clinic (n.d.). *CPTSD (Complex PTSD)*. Retrieved February 14, 2024, from https://my.clevelandclinic.org/health/diseases/24881-cptsd-complex-ptsd

[28] Mental Health America (n.d.). *Is my family dysfunctional?* Retrieved February 15, 2024, from https://screening.mhanational.org/content/my-family-dysfunctional/

[29] Arain, M., Haque, M., Johal, L., Mathur, P., Nel, W., Rais, A., Sandhu, R., & Sharma, S. (2013). Maturation of the adolescent brain. Neuropsychiatric disease and treatment, 9, 449–461. https://doi.org/10.2147/NDT.S39776

[30] Lebow, H. I. (2023, January 21). *How Does Your Body Remember Trauma?* Psych Central. Retrieved February 16, 2024, from https://psychcentral.com/health/how-your-body-remembers-trauma

[31] (2017, July 31). *Eye Movement Desensitization and Reprocessing (EMDR) Therapy*. American Psychological Association. Retrieved February 16, 2024, from https://www.apa.org/ptsd-guideline/treatments/eye-movement-reprocessing

[32] (n.d.). *Try the Butterfly Hug to Help with PTSD Symptoms*. Counseling Connections. Retrieved February 16, 2024, from https://www.counselingconnectionsnm.com/blog/try-the-butterfly-hug-to-help-with-ptsd-symptoms

[33] Aybar, S. (2021, July 21). *4 Somatic Therapy Exercises for Healing from Trauma*. Psych Central. Retrieved February 16, 2024, from https://psychcentral.com/lib/somatic-therapy-exercises-for-trauma#can-you-do-these-at-home

[34] Greenberg, M., Ph.D. (2019, March 31). *Self-Compassion May Foster More Secure Attachment*. Psychology Today. Retrieved February 16, 2024, from https://www.psychologytoday.com/intl/blog/the-mindful-self-express/201903/self-compassion-may-foster-more-secure-attachment?amp

[35] The Attachment Project (2023, April 26). *Be Kind to Yourself: Attachment & Self-Compassion*. Attachment Project. Retrieved February 16, 2024, from https://www.attachmentproject.com/blog/be-kind-to-yourself/

[36] Riopel, L., MsC. (2019, December 9). *17 Self-Awareness Activities and Exercises (+Test)*. Positive Psychology. Retrieved February 17, 2024, from https://positivepsychology.com/self-awareness-exercises-activities-test/#questions

[37] Raypole, C. (2024, January 29). *30 Grounding Techniques to Quiet Distressing Thoughts*. Healthline. Retrieved February 17, 2024, from https://www.healthline.com/health/grounding-techniques

[38] Nunez, K. (2023, April 27). *7 Simple Mindfulness Exercises You Can Easily Fit Into Your Day*. Self. Retrieved February 17, 2024, from https://www.self.com/story/best-mindfulness-exercises

[39] Gotter, A. (2018, April 20). *What Is the 4-7-8 Breathing Technique?* Healthline. Retrieved February 18, 2024, from https://www.healthline.com/health/4-7-8-breathing

[40] Cherry, K., MSEd. (2022, November 8). *Signs of Low Emotional Intelligence*. Verywell Mind. Retrieved February 18, 2024, from https://www.verywellmind.com/signs-of-low-emotional-intelligence-2795958

[41] Lebow, H. I. (2021, June 7). *How Can I Improve Emotional Intelligence (EQ)?* Psych Central. Retrieved February 18, 2024, from https://psychcentral.com/lib/what-is-emotional-intelligence-eq

[42] Robinson, L., Smith, M., M.A.,, Segal, J., Ph.D.,, & Shubin, J. (2023, June 21). *The Benefits of Play for Adults*. Help Guide. Retrieved February 20, 2024, from https://www.helpguide.org/articles/mental-health/benefits-of-play-for-adults.htm

[43] Banks, D. (2024, January 16). *20 Communication Games for Couples to Grow Closer*. Marriage.com. Retrieved February 20, 2024, from https://www.marriage.com/

advice/communication/easy-games-that-can-help-fix-bad-communication/#1_
Twenty_questions

[44] Gould, W. R. (2023, May 26). *Why We Get the Ick, According to Therapists.* Verywell Mind. Retrieved February 20, 2024, from https://www.verywellmind.com/why-we-get-the-ick-according-to-therapists-7501527

[45] National Institute for Play (n.d.). *Play Personalities.* NIF Play. Retrieved February 20, 2024, from https://www.nifplay.org/what-is-play/play-personalities/

[46] Davis, T., M.A., Ph.D., (n.d.). *Relationship Skills.* Berkeley Wellbeing. Retrieved February 20, 2024, from https://www.berkeleywellbeing.com/relationship-skills.html

[47] Pattemore, C. (2021, June 3). *10 Ways to Build and Preserve Better Boundaries.* Psych Central. Retrieved February 20, 2024, from https://psychcentral.com/lib/10-way-to-build-and-preserve-better-boundaries

[48] University of Texas (n.d.). *How Much of Communication Is Nonverbal?* Retrieved February 20, 2024, from https://online.utpb.edu/about-us/articles/communication/how-much-of-communication-is-nonverbal/

[49] West, H., MA., LLP (2022, April 18). *Communication Skills to Build Secure Attachment in Romantic Relationships.* Great Lakes Psychology Group. Retrieved February 20, 2024, from https://www.greatlakespsychologygroup.com/relationships/communication-skills-to-build-secure-attachment-in-romantic-relationships/

[50] Kristensen, S. (2023, March 20). *Toxic VS Healthy Relationship: 7 Important Differences.* Happier Human. Retrieved February 20, 2024, from https://www.happierhuman.com/toxic-vs-healthy-relationship-wa1/

[51] Segal, J., Ph.D., Robinson, L., & Smith, M., M.A. (2023, December 4). *Https://www.Helpguide.Org/articles/relationships-communication/conflict-resolution-skills.Htm.* Help Guide. Retrieved February 20, 2024, from https://www.helpguide.org/articles/relationships-communication/conflict-resolution-skills.htm

[52] Gupta, S. (2023, December 6). *Why Trust Matters in Your Relationship and How to Build It.* Verywell Mind. Retrieved February 20, 2024, from https://www.verywellmind.com/how-to-build-trust-in-a-relationship-5207611

[53] *Emotions Wheel*. Wikimedia Commons. Retrieved February 21, 2024, from https:// commons.wikimedia.org/wiki/File:Emotions_wheel.png

[54] Subic-Wrana, C., Beutel, M. E., Brähler, E., Stöbel-Richter, Y., Knebel, A., Lane, R. D., & Wiltink, J. (2014). How is emotional awareness related to emotion regulation strategies and self-reported negative affect in the general population?. PloS one, 9(3), e91846. https://doi.org/10.1371/journal.pone.0091846

[55] Wilson, C. R., Ph.D. (2021, October 29). *How to Improve Your Empathic Listening Skills: 7 Techniques*. Positive Psychology. Retrieved February 21, 2024, from https:// positivepsychology.com/empathic-listening/

[56] Brandt, A., MFT (2018, March 24). *4 Ways to Be Kinder to Yourself and Build Self-Empathy*. Good Therapy. Retrieved February 21, 2024, from https://www.goodtherapy.org/ blog/4-ways-to-be-kinder-to-yourself-build-self-empathy-0524185/amp/

[57] Coelho, S., CPT (2022, March 9). *12 Journal Prompts for Emotional Health and Awareness*. Psych Central. Retrieved February 21, 2024, from https://psychcentral.com/blog/ journal-prompts-to-heal-emotions

[58] Fritscher, L. (2023, November 20). How to Be Vulnerable. Verywell Mind. Retrieved February 21, 2024, from https://www.verywellmind.com/fear-of-vulnerability-2671820

[59] Deng, C. (2024, January 27). kintsugi. Encyclopedia Britannica. https://www.britannica. com/art/kintsugi-ceramics

Made in the USA
Monee, IL
16 October 2024

67798225R00088